Red Lives

Socialist History 21

Rivers Oram Press
London, Sydney and New York

Editorial Team
Kevin Morgan
Stephen Woodhams
Willie Thompson
David Parker
Mike Waite
David Morgan
Heather Williams
Julie Johnson

Editorial Advisors
Noreen Branson
Rodney Hilton
Eric Hobsbawm
David Howell
Monty Johnstone
Victor Kiernan
David Marquand
Ben Pimlott
Pat Thane

All editorial enquiries to Kevin Morgan, Department of Government, University of Manchester M13 9PL or Kevin.Morgan@man.ac.uk. Reviews enquiries to Stephen Woodhams at SWood18045@aol.com

Published in 2002
by Rivers Oram Press, an imprint of Rivers Oram Publishers Ltd
144 Hemingford Road, London N1 1DE

Distributed in the USA by
New York University Press, 838 Broadway, New York, NY 10003–4183

Distributed in Australia and New Zealand by
UNIReps, University of New South Wales, Sydney, NSW 2052

Set in Garamond by NJ Design Associates
and printed in Great Britain by T.J. International Ltd, Padstow

This edition copyright © 2002 Socialist History Society
The articles are copyright © 2002 Geir Bentzen, Andrew Flinn, Marja Kivisaari, Till Kössler, Tauno Saarela, Margreet Schrevel

No part of this journal may be produced in any form, except for the quotation of brief passages in criticism, without the written permission of the publishers
The right of the contributors to be identified as the authors has been asserted by them in accordance with the Copyright, Designs and Patents Act 1988

British Library Cataloguing in Publication Data
A catalogue record for this publication is available from the British Library
ISBN 1 85489 140 5 (hb)
ISBN 1 85489 141 3 (pb)
ISSN 0969 4331

Contents

Notes on Contributors   v

Editorial   vii

A Dutch Mix of Scouts and Pioneers   1
The *Uilenspiegelclub* children, 1953–1964
Margreet Schrevel

Oppressed Worker or Communist Hero?   11
Characters in Finnish communist magazines of the 1920s
Tauno Saarela

A Party Blocked   24
West German communists between Weimar legacy and
East German policy, 1945–1956
Till Kössler

Cypriot, Indian and West Indian Branches   47
of the CPGB, 1945–1970
An experiment in self-organisation?
Andrew Flinn

Communists are not Born, they are Made   67
The political education system of the French Communist Party
Marja Kivisaari

The *Mot Dag* Association   83
'Leftist academics preaching radical ideas'
Geir Bentzen

Reviews   99

Books to be remembered (4):
Jessica Mitford, *The Making of a Muckraker* (John Saville)   99

Margarita Tupitsyn (ed.), *El Lissitzky, Beyond the abstract cabinet.* 102
Photography, design, collaboration (H. G. A. Hughes)

Stanley Williamson, *Gresford. The anatomy of a disaster* (Keith Gildart) 105

Andrew Forrest, *The Spanish Civil War* (A. D. Atienza)   108

Keith Laybourn and Dylan Murphy, *Under the Red Flag.*   111
A history of communism in Britain (John McIlroy)

Stephen Woodhams, *History in the making. Raymond Williams,*   115
Edward Thompson and radical intellectuals, 1936–1956 (Matthew Worley)

Notes on Contributors

Margreet Schrevel is research officer at the Research and Publications Department of the International Institute of Social History, Amsterdam. She has published the inventory to the Dutch CP archives, a guide to historical sources on Dutch communism and several articles on the postwar communist movement in the Netherlands.

Tauno Saarela is a researcher in the Department of Political History at the University of Helsinki. He has studied Finnish socialist intellectuals and Finnish communism in the inter-war period. He is the author of *Suomalaisen kommunismin synty 1918–1923* (1996), a study of the formative years of Finnish communism.

Till Kössler is completing a dissertation on communism and society in the Ruhr, 1945-1968. From 1997 to 2000 he worked as a researcher on a project at Ruhr-University Bochum on the membership and social composition of the political parties in West Germany 1945-1990.

Andrew Flinn is an editor of *North West Labour History Review* and formerly archivist at the National Museum of Labour History and research officer on the CPGB Biographical Project at the University of Manchester. He completed a PhD on the left in Manchester in the 1930s in 1999.

Marja Kivisaari is a freelance translator and distance translation tutor. In 2000 she completed a PhD on 'The decline of the French Communist Party: the party education system as a brake to change, 1945-90'. She has published a number of articles on the Finnish CP and on the French CP political education system.

Geir Bentzen currently works for the Archive and Library of the Labour

Movement in Oslo and was a research fellow at the University of Oslo from 1998 to 2001. He is working on a doctoral thesis about Norwegian intellectuals and Soviet communism 1917–*c.*1949.

Editorial

In *Socialist History 17* Stefan Berger described some of the obstacles to be overcome in the writing of comparative history, and the benefits to be had from making the attempt. Of the practical obstacles he identified, probably none is more significant than that of acquiring the necessary language skills to keep in touch with work being produced by historians in other countries. As Stefan points out, there is no field of study, not even that of the British labour movement, of which this is not true. But in the study of a phenomenon as little confined by national boundaries as the international communist movement, the benefits of such cross-fertilisation are particularly self-evident. And if it is true that extensive literatures in French or German may be unknown to many British readers, how much truer must that be of studies of communism in the Nordic countries, southern Europe or Latin America, to name but three.

With this in mind, the current issue presents a collection of articles whose subjects will in many cases be relatively unfamiliar to British readers. The articles are derived from the 'People of a Special Mould?' conference on communist biography and prosopography held in Manchester in April of last year. This conference brought together historians of the communist movement from nearly 20 different countries. As well as the nearly 60 academic papers presented, highlights of the weekend included witness seminars on 1956 and internationalism in which key contributions were made by distinguished members of this society (and contributors to this journal) including John Saville, Bill Moore, Alison Macleod and Dennis Ogden. Those attending from outside the UK commented particularly favourably on these witness sessions.

The holding of such an event may itself be regarded as a stimulus to comparative insights. Although only a handful of the papers took an explicitly comparative perspective, it was noticeable how often the discussions at the conference consisted of making connections, drawing parallels, suggesting differences. Stefan Berger in his editorial also suggested that a limitation of much comparative history has been its strongly institutional bias. In the context of communist history, it is certainly true that the focus of the conference on lives and sub-cultures produced a richer and more generous exchange of ideas than some of the arid exchanges of the (ongoing) past.

Of course, the half dozen papers presented here are all of interest and significance in their own right. However, for readers in Britain they have the additional fascination of suggesting linkages and contrasts with movements and events closer to home. Margreet Schrevel's account of the *Uilenspiegelclub* is very much a case in point. It seems that the British Socialist Sunday Schools provided one of the inspirations for the Dutch communist children's organisations, although by the time the *Uilenspiegelclub* came to be formed in the 1950s, probably its nearest British equivalent was the Woodcraft Folk. With its relentless self-criticism and its pseudonyms, in some ways the *Uilenspiegelclub* seems more like the Lenin School than such British prototypes, although as Margreet Schrevel points out, many of its features were common to other youth organisations and its founders were a pair of former scoutmasters only loosely supervised by the party centre. It is a curious combination of influences which the article's title—'A Dutch Mix of Scouts and Pioneers'—captures perfectly.

In very different contexts, Tauno Saarela and Till Kössler are concerned with the tension between indigenous radical cultures and the new ideas and political disciplines of international communism. In both cases, moreover, they describe communist movements that through the sharpest possible polarisation of domestic politics were literally divided into what might be regarded as Soviet and non-Soviet sectors. In Finland after the civil war of 1918, the movement was split between a much constrained indigenous organisation, finally banned in 1930, and a substantial Finnish emigration in Petrograd (later Leningrad). Tauno Saarela traces the tensions between these two worlds of Finnish communism through the unusual medium of the short stories appearing in Finnish communist magazines. He shows that already in the 1920s pressures were felt for heroic and optimistic narratives in a Soviet-style socialist realist mould. Even so, the majority of the stories published continued to offer a more traditional pessimistic representation of the realities of workers' lives under the rule of their enemies.

In postwar Germany, the country itself was divided between the 'two camps'. As Till Kössler shows, this meant that for the communists of the Western sector the issue of subordination to an outside power was posed with peculiar immediacy, as the ruling Socialist Unity Party of the GDR claimed direct jurisdiction over the West German KPD. That essentially was the case for the banning of the KPD in 1956. However, in his very rich and suggestive account Till Kössler shows how these issues of realpolitik were themselves overlain by other tensions, in particular the generational differences which arose with special acuteness after the long hiatus of Nazi rule. Paradoxically, it was the once 'new' communist politics of the Weimar period, heavily shaped by the Soviet example, that in the early postwar period now provided the 'traditional' value systems with which the policies of the returning communist leadership for a time conflicted.

Andrew Flinn and Marja Kivisaari in their articles look at some less familiar aspects of the histories of the British and French communist parties respectively. Taking the example of the CPGB's so-called 'national branches', promoted or at least acquiesced in by the party in the early postwar decades, Andrew Flinn shows how little adapted to a politics of cultural difference were the structures of democratic centralism. Admittedly, he shows that the divisions of opinion on these questions were not at all straightforward, and separate forms of organisation were sometimes regarded—with approval as well as dismay—as a form of marginalisation rather than empowerment. Moreover, political differences over 'revisionism' in international affairs added a further political edge to these divisions, which eventually it proved impossible to reconcile within the framework of the CPGB.

Marja Kivisaari's article also deals with the workings of democratic centralism, focusing on issues of cadre formation and party education in the postwar French Communist Party. She argues convincingly that the unity, discipline and perhaps immobility of the PCF depended fundamentally on a highly developed system of party training that included lengthy residential schools and sometimes study in Moscow. That in turn raises the interesting comparative issue of whether those parties which lacked the resources and perhaps the will for such intensive training, as was certainly the case in Britain, found other ways of maintaining the same central control, or to some extent found it slipping away from them.

In our final article, Geir Bentzen describes the intriguing history of *Mot Dag*, an association of young, privileged left-wing rebels which emerged in Norway after the First World War. With their elitism, disdain for commerce, sympathy for Bolshevism and affinity with the Norwegian labour movement, the motdagists suggest numerous parallels with their contemporaries in other countries. Though they are not drawn out in the article itself, the possible parallels with the British case are immediately apparent. For example, it would be fascinating to compare how far the *motdagists'* changing perceptions of Soviet socialism mirrored those of left-wing or technocratic Fabian socialists, and whether the British welfare state also shows something of the same ideological lineage.

If readers have suggestions for future articles on international themes, we would be very pleased to hear of them.

Note

This conference was funded by ESRC award number R000 237924.

A Dutch Mix of Scouts and Pioneers
The *Uilenspiegelclub* children, 1953–1964

Margreet Schrevel

The Dutch children's organisation *Uilenspiegelclub* emerged in 1953, lasted until 1964 and contributed to the upbringing of about three thousand children. *Uilenspiegelclub* was the youngest scion of the Dutch postwar communist family. As such it deliberately tried to impose a communist mentality on its members. This poses some interesting questions: What did this look like in practice? How was the ideal communist child supposed to behave? What sort of knowledge and attitudes did club children learn, and how do they look back on this now? In what ways did the club distinguish itself from other youth organisations and how did it relate to official party ideology? What made it different from other youth movements? To find some answers, I have researched the club's and Communist Party archives at the International Institute of Social History (IISH) in Amsterdam and interviewed former members of both organisations.[1]

The idea of organising and training children within the communist movement is almost as old as the movement itself. At its birth in 1909, the Dutch Communist Party (CPN) with its 419 members was simply too small to be active in this field.[2] An initiative to found Communist Sunday Schools, inspired by British examples, was taken as early as 1919 but the initiator, Andries van Gool, died before his project could take shape. Only in the 1920s and 1930s, when CP membership had grown to some 5000, did children's groups or Pioneer groups prove capable of survival. These Dutch Pioneers were tiny relatives of their great Soviet counterpart. Their groups were named after celebrities like Rosa Luxemburg, Molotov or Clara Zetkin and had some thirty members each. On Sunday mornings the children came together to play and dance. In summertime they camped out at the seaside.

During the Second World War, a tremendous sympathy for the Dutch communist resistance had grown and the CPN emerged as a respectable party, with ten per cent of the vote in the 1946 general elections and some 500,000 members. The CPN could now reach out and gave birth to all kind of subsidiary organisations to nurse its members from the cradle to the grave. One of these was the *Nederlandse Pioniersbond* (NPB), a children's group for eight- to fourteen-year-olds, established in 1949 along similar lines to the Pioneers in other European countries. However, the *Pioniersbond* did not leave any marks in the history of Dutch communism and died four years later. As with earlier party initiatives, a continual lack of appropriate officers/instructors and training materials for children made itself felt. It was now understood that these matters should be approached from another angle.

In 1950, the party initiated a new family magazine called *Uilenspiegel*. It was named after the hero of a picturesque novel which was very popular in the Low Countries. No doubt the name of this famous rogue was chosen for its associations with humour, love of freedom, youth and vigour. The magazine looked like any other specimen of the popular press. It had a doctor's column, chess column, recipes and luxurious fashion from Rome or Paris. Anita Ekberg featured on its front pages along with two *cabaretiers* from the Chinese People's Republic. Its communist background was to remain concealed. Children had their own pages in *Uilenspiegel* entitled 'We are young and we feel great'. They could submit letters, small stories or drawings to a special editorial board of peers. Out of these columns for the young, the *Uilenspiegelclub* was born in October 1953. Its target group was eight- to fifteen-year-olds. Two journalists from *Uilenspiegel*, Peter Boezeman and Henk Nijman, further elaborated this idea and eventually became the club's leaders. Both were fresh postwar members of the party, and no old cadres whatsoever were active in the club.

The club's profile

The *Uilenspiegelclub* lasted from October 1953 until the beginning of 1964 and developed from a magazine-bound club into a hobby club and camping organisation. It had 271 members in March 1954, 2000 in 1957. Membership as a whole, from the beginning to the end, totalled around 3000. Its stronghold was Amsterdam, but at some time the club had fifteen branches throughout the country. No contribution fee was required. Activities took place in party buildings, the budget derived from that of the *Uilenspiegel* magazine.

Many aspects of the *Uilenspiegelclub*'s profile were imitated or derived from other youth organisations. Interestingly enough, the melody of the club's favourite song was identical to the social-democrat *Arbeiders Jeugd Centrale* club song; only the text was different. Traditional Dutch children's songs completed the repertoire. The club's marketing and advertising were clearly influenced by commercial practice. Ceremonies and rituals such as greeting the flag every morning during camp were taken over from the Pioneers' clubs in Eastern Europe. The *Uilenspiegelclub*'s club tie was yellow, not red as one would expect, and this colour was explicitly chosen to avoid the image of sectarianism. Apart from the club tie, there were several insignia to be earned. Like the international scouting movement and the Soviet Pioneers, the children were organised in small groups of eight to ten. But unlike the Scouts, these small *Uilenspiegel* groups were led by older children: the 'Great Owls', who were around fifteen years old. They performed all kinds of educational tasks, and among other responsibilities they cooked, took care of the hurt and the homesick, initiated play, and cleaned up.

The club's children filled an enormous number of magazines—*Uilenspiegel* itself was just one of them—with their small stories, letters, drawings and jokes. They could earn bonus points and save these up for presents (games like mikado and traditional Dutch children's books). Each new member received a certificate with a code printed on it to be able to decipher the 'secret' message in every week's *Uilenspiegel* magazine. The novice chose a pseudonym for him or herself as an exclusive club alias. Thus, 'Stalina' and 'Galina Ulianova' turned out to be clubmates of 'Audrey Hepburn' and 'Romy Schneider'. The club also participated in communist party festivals and feasts. The results of the children's hobby work were shown there and children of party members were taken care of in a sort of nursery. The club children performed in pantomimes and plays, they learned how to peel potatoes and how to repair a flat tyre. They did quizzes and performed folk dancing. During club camps they performed sports, hiked and organised a treasure hunt. An elementary knowledge of nature, tying knots and how to use a compass was required.

Active club members could be selected to visit a camp in Eastern Germany, Czechoslovakia or Hungary. About fifteen children went there annually by train or plane—an extraordinary luxury at that time, one that was paid for by the foreign host. In these camps, apart from the normal activities such as hiking and folk dancing, the children went on excursions with a political theme: the Berlin Wall, or a former nazi concentration camp. They came back full of good intentions: 'I will tell my fellow children at school that socialism is much better than capitalism', one of them wrote.[3]

The ideal communist child?

The population of the *Uilenspiegelclub* consisted of school-age children from communist families, mostly of skilled labour background. The club did not recruit neglected children from the backstreet areas. No attention was paid to the personal history and domestic situation of the pupils. The club's children were born during or shortly after the Second World War and many of them had parents suffering from war trauma. But this was a subject to avoid and in fact parents were not really welcome in the club. Nevertheless, they had great confidence in the club, which offered their children an opportunity to entertain themselves among soul mates. During the Cold War, communist families lived in an atmosphere of resistance which echoed the wartime underground. The club partly compensated for the communist family's isolated position in society. Among communists the wartime attitude of militancy was continued and was implanted in children of very young age. Typical rules of conduct were: work hard, control yourself and guard secrecy.[4] In the *Uilenspiegelclub*, with its aliases and secret codes, this way of looking at life was intensified.

A club child never did nothing. A farm landscape with windmills made out of matches was to be created for an exhibition at a party festival; a group worked at it for seven months on Sundays. During a hiking tour in the woods, some sculpture of sand had to be erected collectively to promote the sense of togetherness. Two hundred metres of paper *guirlande* had to be produced by hand for the party congress and dozens of wooden chairs had to be sandpapered and painted for the same event. After every session of the club, each member had to make a report. Children were to criticise each other frequently and to engage in self-criticism. The group perspective was paramount: 'individualism' was not tolerated. Children excelling in some respect were regarded with suspicion and in danger of being called vain. During the sessions of criticism and self-criticism, any unpleasant behaviour was defined as 'individualism', the greatest enemy to the club spirit. For example: a boy buying himself a lemonade while the group was supposed to be on its way to a hiking tour was severely criticised. A girl was expelled from a panel altogether because she left a meeting in favour of her dancing lessons. By the leadership she was branded as 'the prototype of the wronged sectarian girl'. Others were 'sarcastic, which is un-communist', 'too soft' or, even worse, had 'dictatorial inclinations'.[5] If a group had decided to play soccer, the two or three individuals who preferred to sit down and watch had to comply with the group and join in the game. Sessions of criticism and self-criticism were held after every meeting, even daily during the camping weeks. Criticism and self-criticism were regarded as a sublime form of friendship. But no one had any professional experience in this field and many former pupils remember these sessions as harsh, rude and embarrassing. Moreover, the small adult leaders' collective was itself very uncommunicative. Critical remarks from the pupils about the organisation were rejected without discussion.

Girls and boys were treated as equals, but gender differences were acknowledged without discussion. Thus, the girls would organise a dolls' fashion show and sew dolls' clothes; the boys would build the *décor* for it. Girls predominated in the club, most of all in the Great Owl echelon. This was seen as proof that girls were by nature inclined to nursing and mothering young children. Special days were celebrated—Boys' Day and Girls' Day—for the sexes to attend to each others' wants, give each other small presents, do the cooking and all other household jobs. The existence of homosexuality was denied. Some incidents prove that it did exist; these were concealed and it was hoped that the party leadership would not notice. Naturally the children, especially the older Great Owls, tended to fall in love with each other, but they were not allowed to show this in public. It would be condemned as 'individualism'. On the other hand, regardless of their affiliation, a taboo on openly being in love was common in other Dutch youth organisations as well. And even so, many pupils met their partner for life in the *Uilenspiegelclub*.

Cleanliness was very important. Every now and then the pupils' feet and hands were checked. Filthy language and foul play were seen as serious misdemeanours. If a pupil did utter some incorrect words, it was supposed that he or she had picked these up at school. Every day, every hour was organised in minute detail and for every single activity a responsible person was put in charge. Nothing happened just for pleasure or fun: there had to be an additional goal, a perspective, a learning objective to every activity. A hiking tour had some hidden educational aspects; during a treasure hunt perceptions had to be trained, or children were meant to learn that it is very important to work together and stick to one's word.

The club thus tried to breed the ideal communist child. This child was well-organised and disciplined. It acted only in the interest of the group and neglected its own ambitions, talents and feelings. Self-sacrifice was its prevailing attitude. It was clean and tidy. It had a vast knowledge of nature and it knew how to camp, how to cook and do odd jobs. It knew that it was imperfect and it could interpret criticism as a sign of friendship. It had a great sense of responsibility for other people's well-being. It had not the faintest idea of teenage rebellion. It could keep a secret and it was aware that being a communist was being something different, something to be proud of and to keep silent about at the same time.

Some pupils rebelled against the club's excessive organisation and discipline. They would leave the club after a short while, pretending to have too much homework to do. Some of them honestly stated the reason for their abdication: 'during the club camp, we had do something every single minute.

Just a bit more freedom wouldn't harm anybody...' 'The club has too many similarities with Scouting and militarism'. 'The way criticism is practised is offensive and the leaders spare each other'.[6] If they were absent more than three times without a good reason they would be expelled anyway. But others felt inspired and stayed to become member of the elite Great Owls. Rethinking their past now, they say they learned how to organise, how to behave in a group, how to be generous to others, how to make something out of nothing. They still foster their sense of being different and having a mission to accomplish. They feel their cultural awareness increased during their club years. They emphasise the great measure of freedom and responsibility they enjoyed. Most of all, they appreciate having been treated as adults, not as the children they actually were. As one of them put it: 'The club was important for your cultural knowledge. We went to good films. I started reading Zola at sixteen. Not many children had learned about such things at home. The idea of collectivity attracted me most of all. I have learned to organise there, to make something out of nothing. I liked the way we treated each other. They listened to what I said, at a very early age I became a group leader and it worked out well!'[7]

Leadership and ideology

Despite the *Uilenspiegelclub*'s striking characteristics, a superficial comparison with other youth organisations reveals some surprising similarities. There was a strong resemblance, not only in activities and outward appearance, but in aims as well. The Scout movement, church-based organisations, the social democrats and the communists, regardless of their nationality, likewise applauded handiwork, love of nature, friendship and companionship. There was, however, quite a divergence in the basic assumptions of these youth organisations. Protestants encountered God in nature, whereas catholics in the woods learned to act in 'catholic awareness'. Developing friendship feelings was the main issue in social democrats' eyes. For the communists, nature added up to solidarity and comradeship. Every single youth organisation developed its own style and appearance, but in themselves dance ceremonies, greeting the flag, scarves and insignia were worldwide phenomena. Only the form and colours were different.

What gave the *Uilenspiegelclub* its singularity then? In the end, this can all be traced back to ideology. Within a few years, the club developed from a relatively open organisation towards a rigorously dogmatic one. This was perhaps an attempt to take root firmly and pacify the ever-dissatisfied party. For although the *Uilenspiegelclub* was an exclusively communist organisation, its relationship with the party was tricky from beginning to end. The CPN felt but little responsibility for the club's wellbeing and hardly intervened in its policy at all. The party's reticence can be explained by its continuous scarcity of cadres. In the 1950s, when the popularity of the CPN had drastically declined compared to the initial postwar years, the party had to make the most of the few cadres available and so a hobby club for children had little priority. There were no party officials in charge of the *Uilenspiegelclub*. There was hardly any advertising for the club in inner party circles, though some leading party families did send their children to the club.

Initially, the club did get the benefit of the doubt; it fitted into the tradition of children's organisation advocated by the Soviet Union. Moreover, the postwar CPN envied social democracy with its elaborate system of sub-organisations for all age groups and categories. The communists did their best to establish a second 'red family' after this fashion. At first the club was quite popular. But in 1964 the party forced the club to disband. This decision was linked with the 1963 Sino-Soviet conflict, when the Dutch party pledged to be 'neutral' and 'autonomous'. It officially broke with the Soviet Union and all party sub-organisations were forced to do the same. This resulted in a serious conflict between the party itself and those of its own organisations which had direct links with the Soviet Union, such as their publishers house and the Society of Dutch Friends of the Soviet Union. The *Uilenspiegelclub* had tied itself ideologically to the Soviet Union and thus, in 1963, it turned out to be in the wrong position. The club leaders had tried to live up to party standards as they saw these and until 1963 followed party policy scrupulously, but in the end they won no sympathy by this.

Thus, eventually, ideological and political dissent was the *coup de grâce* for the club in 1964, but it came at a time when death for the club was near anyway. Its downfall kept pace with an increasing emphasis on ideological rooting and orientation towards the Soviet Union. At the height of this trend, in 1959, the decline in membership had already become irreversible. In the credentials of the club in 1953, play, handicraft and friendship were foremost. Children should learn to like helping elderly people and animals. No mention was made of 'class consciousness' or similar terms. In 1957, the club's main aim was defined as developing responsibility, self-criticism and helpfulness. By 1958 this had become 'breeding young people with a talent to organise, useful and militant people, able to work jointly in the party or other progressive organisations'.[8] Marxism had become fundamental as a direction for life and a starting-point for all activities. Free expression was dismissed as 'too individualistic'.

More and more, the club leaders had addressed themselves to the Soviet Union for guidance in their work. An important source of inspiration was the pedagogy of the Ukrainian teacher Anton Makarenko (1888–1939); his main work *The Road to Life* had earlier been published in Dutch translation by the CPN publishing company.[9] Makarenko had worked with abandoned children during the 1920s, a time of famine in the Ukraine. He strongly advocated the training of team spirit, group work and collective ownership. The sense of belonging to a group was enhanced, in Makarenko's view, by showing respect to children and giving them responsibility. Thus, the worst conceivable punishment for a child would be rejection by the group. Makarenko's basic principles were friendship, collectivity, discipline, criticism and self-criticism, play and handicraft as vehicles for learning. The teachings of Makarenko were prescribed as subject-matter to club members around 1958.

By 1959 the club's ideological petrification was complete, as demonstrated by the institution of a twenty-page 'programme of demands' as a condition of membership. All kinds of knowledge, ranging from the history of the labour movement to cooking on a stove, were henceforth tested in exams. In the same year the favourite club song, with its friendly aura, was reworded into something militant, stressing the need for self-criticism. Interestingly enough, some of the club's manifestations, such as criticism and self-criticism, were shunned by the party itself—as by all other Dutch communist organisations—as too rigid.

Unparallelled in the youth movement was the club's practice that fifteen- to sixteen-year-old children guided the younger ones. The adult club leaders remained in the background to guard policy and ideology. In daily clublife a hand-picked body of children laid down the law, children who were regarded as experienced and esteemed collaborators. Here, the idea of the vanguard, central to communist doctrine, had materialised.

The club's ideology and politics emanated from its twin leadership, Peter Boezeman and Henk Nijman. They were party members, but no seniors; they lacked an established reputation in the party. They were both of Roman Catholic background and they had previously been scoutmasters. Within the small leadership collective—Boezeman and his wife, Nijman, and a few nearly grown-up inner-circle club members—relations had become more and more intense; love and hatred flourished, triangular and extra-marital bonds were woven and a wedding partner interchanged. It may be bold to assume a connection between these processes of ideological and oyster-like sexual enclosure. The subject of sexual and family relationships within communist organisations in western countries is an unexplored and potentially rich field.

Fatal lack of appeal

Initially, the *Uilenspiegelclub* was a rather informal, seemingly apolitical organisation. Gradually, the club grafted itself onto Soviet ideology and educational practice, and did so in such a strict manner that its position within the Dutch communist movement became more and more isolated. The CPN had regarded the club with scepticism from the beginning. Play and hobbywork had no priority in the party's view and it assigned no cadres to coach the club. In the end, the party forced the club to disband as ideologically and politically suspect.

But even without this final intervention, the club had already pined away from its own lack of appeal. Partly, this reflected a more general decline in popularity of communism at the time. Moreover, in its unattractiveness during the 1960s, the *Uilenspiegelclub* was in no way unique. All Dutch youth organisations suffered from a decrease in membership. In a time of increasing consumption, beat groups and Cliff Richard films, there was no attraction in folk dance, a knowledge of funghi, worshipping communist war veterans or sessions of criticism and self-criticism. Only a small group of children within the club, the Great Owls, held a different opinion. They felt part of a cultural and moral elite. This feeling of exclusiveness had been fostered at home and was reinforced by the club's use of aliases and its attitude of secrecy. The vanguard of Great Owls was charged with serious duties and difficult tasks. The fact that they were children was more or less denied. They became used to hard work according to plan, cleanliness, discipline and effacing the self. Nowadays, they still emphasise the amount of knowledge and number of skills—and friends—they gathered there. They felt safe among soul mates with whom they shared feelings of exclusiveness and a perspective of future happiness.

Thus, ideological petrification and orientation towards the Soviet Union account for the club's isolated position within the communist movement. It also clarifies the club's lack of appeal to children living in Dutch society in the 1960s. But this same ideology, for a small group of children, generated and reinforced a mentality of exclusiveness and missionary zeal, in which their feeling of being treated like grown-ups was crucial.

Notes

1. For a review see M. Schrevel, 'Romy Schneider en Stalina samen in een club: de communistische kinderorganisatie Uilenspiegelclub 1953–1964', *Tijdschrift voor Sociale Geschiedenis*, vol. 25, no. 1 (1999) pp.1–24.
2. The *Communistische Partij van Nederland* (CPN) dates from 1909, when the *Sociaal-Democratische Partij* (SDP) was founded as a split-away from social democracy.

Membership of the Dutch CP from 1909 till 1990 is reviewed by M. Schrevel in G. Voerman (eds), *De communistische erfenis. Bibliografie en bronnen betreffende de CPN* (Amsterdam, 1997), pp.164–70.
3. *Uilenspiegelclub* archive, International Institute for Social History, Amsterdam, (hereafter IISH), no.53.
4. This process of prolonged war mentality is convincingly described by J. Withuis, *Opoffering en heroïek. De mentale wereld van een communistische vrouwenorganisatie in naoorlogs Nederland 1946–1976* (Meppel, 1990).
5. *Uilenspiegelclub* archive, IISH, no. 13, 31, 33.
6. *Uilenspiegelclub* archive, IISH, no. 32, 33.
7. Interview with Mrs. Carla van Buuren, 9 September 1998.
8. *Uilenspiegelclub* archive, IISH, no.29.
9. A. Makarenko, *De weg naar het leven* (Amsterdam, 1949–1952); J. Bowen, *Soviet education. Makarenko and the years of experiment* (Madison, 1962).

Oppressed Worker or Communist Hero?
Characters in Finnish communist magazines of the 1920s

Tauno Saarela

The communist movement was intended by its proponents to create new people with new values, attitudes and manners. Guidelines for these new people were given in the instructions on the tasks of a party member but also by presenting models for members and supporters.[1] Such models were, for instance, Karl Liebknecht, Rosa Luxemburg and V.I. Lenin who were praised for having been energetic, unyielding and inspiring. Identification with them was, however, not easy—Lenin, for example, was regarded as a genius and infallible, which was probably not expected from every communist.[2]

More ordinary models for these new people were produced in fiction and its characters. In the 1920s, communist literature was not particularly committed to furthering the creation of communist heroes. Earlier socialist literature had, however, presented models to be adopted, such as Pavel Vlasov in Maxim Gorky's *Mother*, and Ernest Everhard and Martin Eden in Jack London's works. The Russian civil war heroes of Alexander Fadeev and Dmitri Furmanov, and Gleb Chumalov in Fjodor Gladkov's novel *Cement*, which described the era of socialist reconstruction, were also inspiring characters.

All these heroes went through a process of development—'through suffering and humiliation, through struggle, through ordeals, through weaknesses experienced, understood and conquered'—and surmounted obstacles before them. They did not, however, dedicate themselves to the communist cause as totally as Nikolai Ostrovsky's Pavel Korchagin was to do in the 1930s. In other respects too they were more complicated characters.[3]

These books and their heroes created a model for writing short stories about workers and communists, as did the traditions of working-class literature in every country.[4] This article considers what kind of working-class characters were presented in Finnish communist literary magazines in the 1920s.

Finnish communism and its literary magazines

Finnish communism was born in two countries, in Soviet Russia and in

Finland. The leaders of an abortive revolution escaped to Soviet Russia in spring 1918 and founded the Finnish Communist Party (from 1920 onwards the Communist Party of Finland) in August. The party was captivated by the hope of immediate world revolution and yielded itself to the new ideas of communism. It was forbidden in Finland and its central organs were located outside the country up to the autumn of 1944. The party, however, cooperated with various organs and persons in Finland.

Within Finland, Finnish communism was formed around the Socialist Workers' Party which was founded in the spring 1920 and banned in August 1923. After that, Finnish communism in Finland was organised in various electoral, political and cultural organisations until they were banned during the summer of 1930.

Finnish communism was a mixture of new communist ideas and the inherited traditions of the Finnish labour movement. At the ideological level both those in Soviet Russia and those in Finland were willing to accept new communist ideas, but in daily politics—under the threat of imprisonment and the dissolution of their organisations, while trying to win the support of workers and peasants—those in Finland preferred to follow their own labour traditions. For the party leaders in Leningrad or Moscow this gave rise to constant demands for ideological orthodoxy. Discontinuity of speech and activities was characteristic for Finnish communism.[5]

The literary magazine was not a communist invention in the Finnish labour movement, and such a weekly had come out in Helsinki in 1902–6. In the 1920s, however, the enthusiasm for literary magazines was much greater. The Finnish communist youth published two literary weeklies: *Liekki*, which came out in Helsinki in 1923–30 and *Revontulet* which appeared in Oulu between 1926 and1930. Besides these, the pictorial magazine *Itä ja Länsi* and the spring and Christmas periodicals *Rynnäkköön* and *Nuoren Työläisen Joulu*, as well as the handwritten papers of the youth associations, all published fiction.

The communist youth founded literary magazines for many reasons. As early as 1916–17 there had been discussions among them about creating their own organ for workers' literary needs, but because of the Civil War and its aftermath the achievement of this objective had to wait until 1923. The magazines were also founded to raise money for the daily newspapers. The main reason for their publishing, however, was the challenge presented to the labour movement by commercial popular culture with its popular fiction, magazines and film. The literary magazines of the communist youth were intended to prevent the young workers from committing themselves to 'cheap and bad entertainment' and to keep them in the sphere of the movement's influence.

The magazines published texts of those authors who were of labour origins, wrote of workers' life or displayed sympathy for them or their movement. These writers included the Russians Maxim Gorky and Lev Tolstoi, the Americans Jack London and Upton Sinclair, the Frenchmen Anatole France and Henri Barbusse, and the Dane Martin Andersen Nexö. The famous short story writers Anton Tsekhov, Guy de Maupassant and Mark Twain were popular, too. New Soviet fiction was also introduced on the pages of the magazines, although as the example of Mikhail Zoshchenko indicates, they did not necessarily favour pro-communist writers.

Foreign writers were not the only ones to contribute to the magazines. Finnish young communists also wrote plenty of short stories. Among these authors were young writers who had already 'established themselves' by publishing a book or two and the editors of the magazines, as well as other less known writers. The magazines also organised writing contests in order to generate stories. In most cases the writers had only an elementary education behind them. As a result, they were less eager to theorise about literature and its tasks than to write short stories intended to tell how the workers lived and fought in the maelstrom of life.[6]

The oppressed worker

Inspiring communist characters were thus almost entirely missing in the short stories published in the magazines; the first numbers were, rather, full of stories describing the hardships of workers' lives. Agricultural work in particular was portrayed as toil which brought no improvement to one's life. Factory work, with its long and fatiguing working days, tight discipline and occasional fatal accidents, was no better. Even logging, characterised in Finnish literature as having romantic features, was exposed for its tough conditions.[7] In such circumstances, the workers could take no professional pride in their work.

The short stories also told of other hardships suffered by the workers. Unemployment and poverty meant that young working women ended up in the streets as prostitutes, families were ejected from their homes, the elderly and orphans were neglected, and innocent people were imprisoned.[8] These hardships were not presented in order to show the workers overcoming them; rather, they broke down under them—the characters could die, end up as beggars, drunkards or strike-breakers.[9] Even glimpses of a brighter future could be destroyed—an escaping political refugee is shot at the border; a young worker studying singing dies at the point of success.[10]

This kind of story of workers' sufferings was typical of the literary tradition of the Finnish labour movement, which was very strongly influenced by realism and naturalist determinism. Typical of the early Finnish realism was the passivity of the characters, their negative and pessimistic feelings—in some stories the only solution was death. These aspects were readily accepted in the labour movement at the turn of the twentieth century.[11] The hard experiences after the Civil War in 1918 and the continuous political discrimination in the 1920s may have strengthened the negative tone of the stories.

According to this tradition it was believed that the dark colours of the stories would not only increase the knowledge of the injustice of existing society but also touch readers' emotions and strengthen their hatred towards it; the hardships were supposed to toughen people. This kind of story of sufferings can be found in Finnish communist magazines throughout the decade, despite the declared aim of the magazines that their stories should broaden the world view of their readers and strengthen their will for action.[12] However, it was not until the autumn of 1928 that these stories of sufferings were actually criticised in *Liekki*. While it was accepted that they portrayed the real life of working people, they were also held to diminish it by not telling anything of the bravery of the workers' attitude towards that life. *Liekki*'s critic recommended that the darkness of the stories should be brightened by the great future that lay before the working class.[13]

In the summer of 1929 Ludvig Kosonen, the editor of *Liekki* and the only person in the communist youth movement who tried to explain the value of literature in the struggle of the workers, said that such stories of workers' sufferings belonged to an earlier period when the working class was weak and unorganised and set its sights on attaining equal status with the bourgeoisie. In the 1920s, on the other hand, the working class was trying to reach the dominant position in society. The task of proletarian art was to kindle emotions for the great cause and goal of the working class. Along with depictions of misery, the stories should therefore tell about 'the magnificent heroism, the infallible belief in the future and indomitable fighting spirit' of the working class—the art should be a standard-bearer for the future.[14]

Kosonen himself, however, did not at that time present any characters who would have filled these demands, but rather described unheroic members of the working class. He even thought that the ideal persons did not yet exist.[15] It was only in the early 1930s, when Kosonen had escaped to the Soviet Union, that he published a book which told of the youth movement in Helsinki as he would have liked it to have been.[16]

The villains

The stories of workers' sufferings did not present positive heroes but rather expressed criticism of existing society and introduced its 'villains'. The employers were often described as immoral and unscrupulous persons, who, for instance, when work accidents happened were worried only about the interruption in production.[17] Factory owners and their sons, foremen, farm owners and also priests were depicted as seducing, even raping, young working women.[18] The villains also included the authorities: a judge could sentence a woman he had seduced in prison for child-murder;[19] a successful and respected undertaker was revealed as a bootlegger;[20] a sawmill owner was planning to burn his timberyard and to frame the strikers as victims.[21] And the rival youth associations were connected with drinking, fighting and a generally indecent life.[22]

The stories of the injustices of society were often fictitious but sometimes they came quite close to actual incidents. After the banning of the Socialist Youth League and the arrest of dozens of its members at the end of 1925, *Liekki* published a story in which a 17-year-old boy, after a long time in custody, is accused of plotting high treason and is sentenced to prison for a year and a half. According to the story, the only crime committed by the young man was that he wanted to study in the labour organisation at the end of his long working day.[23]

Moral disapproval was not the only way to react against injustice. Violation of workers' civil rights produced stories mocking the institutions—courts of justice and political police—and persons behind these offences, as well as their ways of thinking. Armas Äikiä, the future member of the Terijoki government and the leading Stalinist in aesthetic discussions within the Finnish communist movement after the Second World War, placed his story in 'Benitoland' where 300 young workers are arrested because the newspapers have written about their plans for a bomb attack. The boxes presented as evidence and believed to contain dynamite turn out to contain ski wax. Nevertheless, the youngsters are sentenced to prison because they have betrayed the state 'by claiming that ski wax is dynamite and thus misled the political police and the court and ridiculed them which is the same as preparation for the revolution'.[24]

Stories ridiculing the political police, or 'okhrana', as it was called according to its Russian predecessor, were also common. It was usual to tell how its actions were based on rumours and misunderstandings. In one of the stories some 'okhrana' detectives overhear someone in the Helsinki labour hall talking about obtaining arms for the following Saturday. On that day the detectives form a cordon around the labour hall, but find out that what they had heard was the members of a theatre group talking about their next play.[25]

This kind of story was written in order to challenge the legitimacy of the authorities and the whole existing order of society. Although they urged the working youth to the same kind of mockery, they seldom presented actual humorous characters themselves.

Labour movement as hero

There were no individual heroes in the early stories; the hero was, rather, the whole labour movement. Thus there were many stories about young working men or women who were saved from ruining their lives by joining a labour youth association.[26] Accordingly, the labour movement was in some stories described in terms of an actual place of solidarity which served as a counterbalance to their gloomy working life—a place where the workers could study, have social evenings and spend their leisure time, without having to confront the outside world.[27] For instance, the youth associations used to spend their summer weekends in their own (hired) places, perhaps on nearby islands, to which the youth would make excursions by rowing boat. In this respect the stories did not follow the instructions of the communist movement, which demanded that their organisations should orientated towards activity; they should not be places where people only spent time together.

Although the labour movement was portrayed as of great importance, its heroic qualities were nevertheless very much understated. The stories in the magazines very seldom described the strength of the labour movement, and heroic overtones were much more frequent in their poems. In the early years the stories portrayed even strikes in pessimistic tones—the strikes failed and the workers might become strikebreakers.[28] There were, however, sometimes glimpses of class-conscious activities; for instance the children of the striking workers throwing stones at strikebreakers.[29]

The determination and the success of the striking workers became more evident in the latter half of the decade[30]—perhaps as a reflection of large strikes in the country.[31] The collective appeal of the labour movement also became more commonly portrayed in the last years of the decade. A group of young workers spending their weekends on an island could, for example, persuade the young men of a nearby village to change their attitude towards the working youth and join the ranks of the movement.[32] Nevertheless, the stories were not particularly written in order to encourage organisational activities, even though these were regarded as very important within the communist movement. Therefore there were no stories by those living in Finland about creating a workplace organisation. Only a few articles originating from the Soviet Union and America told of workers who established cells in the factories.[33]

Lone heroes

The literary tradition of the Finnish labour movement was not entirely devoid of positive, inspiring heroes. Some writers had in the 1910s presented characters whose model was Spartacus, the rebellious Roman slave.[34] By the

1920s such heroes were untypical, although half-documentary, half-fictional stories of courageous fighting down to the last bullet in the Civil War could be seen as a continuation of the same type.[35]

Such heroes were more likely to be placed in other parts of the world, and young Finnish writers made up adventure stories about Russian revolutionaries and rebels in Latin America.[36] These stories were written in a different style, possibly copying those numerous adventure stories originating from America, Britain, Germany, Sweden, and the Soviet Union. These stories were very common in the Finnish communist youth magazines, even though adventure stories in general were dismissed as trash in the same magazines.[37]

The most colourful of these stories takes place in a fictional Latin American state, Nicazuela, where poor *vaqueros* (cowboys), farm labourers and the workers of a few cities rise in rebellion. This event is so surprising that the president of the country dies of astonishment. The rebellion is, however, suppressed by a general who creates a dictatorship and puts the rebels in prison camps. In this phase of the story the hero, a Finnish seaman and ex-Red Guardist, enters the stage. He escapes from a prison camp with a native friend of his and, posing as an American, he moves to the capital of the country where he spreads the rumour that the dictator of the country has disappeared. At the end of the story the Finn is sitting in the office of the prime minister asking him to grant an amnesty to all political prisoners. His demands are supported by the announcement that the dictator is his prisoner and by the explosions sounding all around the city. The demands are, of course, accepted.[38]

This story presented a hero who was capable of both solving problems without difficulty and getting others to follow him. It is, however, doubtful whether the text was written in order to inspire readers to similar deeds—it was too unreal for that. This story was, more likely, intended to make fun of a common mould of popular fiction in the then young nation state of Finland. According to that mould, the Finns were an extraordinary people, no matter what part of the world they were to be found in.[39]

This kind of 'heroic determination' and 'brave action' from a few individual men was criticised in the magazines.[40] It did, however, influence the stories which took place on Finnish soil and whose themes had connections with the Finnish labour movement. *Liekki*, for instance, published in March 1927 a story where an employer of a lumber site hires a notorious fighter and bootlegger to prevent the organisational work of a trade union agitator. This plan comes to nothing because the agitator is a former boxer and wrestler; he knocks out the disturber and continues his speech, with the result that 100 per cent organisation is established.[41]

In a story published in the first album of the Union of Proletarian Writers in 1929 the workers are inspired by the example of the hero. The story describes a young communist working in a saw mill. During his lunch hours and spare time he participates eagerly in discussions and begins to win support. One morning he does not come to work, and it is revealed that he has been arrested by the okhrana. This piece of news makes the workers stop their work, leave the saw mill and march to the labour hall, singing the *International*.[42]

The promise of an active movement inspired by an individual communist was not always thought so obvious and a young worker dedicating himself to the class struggle could also be somewhat problematic as a model. In a story published in *Liekki* in summer 1928 a young man wanted by the police comes to the youth meeting in the labour hall because it is his turn to give a lecture. In his speech he argues for the vanguard which is prepared for the revolution and can lead the masses towards it. When the police arrive at the hall, he does not try to escape, but explains to others that prison is a school for revolutionaries.[43] This story is a good example of how the Finnish communists had difficulties in solving the problem of being a true communist and maintaining the movement's and personal possibilities for action.

Class struggle and love

Although in the Finnish communist movement love stories of the popular fiction variety were regarded as trash, *Revontulet* in particular published dozens of them in translation.[44] Even the young communists wrote stories which told of the relations between young working men and women. In the early years of *Liekki* the stories tried to convince the reader that 'the working girl of one's dreams' would be found 'in the army of the fighters'.[45] In other words, it was possible to unite love, family life and activities in the labour movement if the aspirations of the two people involved were alike. Participation in the class struggle was usually regarded as a condition for living together. These stories did not reflect great passion but rather preached in favour of comradeship and against jealousy and possessiveness.[46]

The possibility of uniting love and activity in the movement was not a notion shared by all writers. Some of them created characters—usually young men—who decided to give up their beloved in order to dedicate their lives to revolutionary work. These persons also tried to convince others that the fight for socialist ideas was more important than home and family.[47] This kind of story became more common in the last years of the decade and might have anticipated the puritanical heroes of 1930s Soviet literature for whom the private sphere was nothing in comparison with the public.

In the Finnish stories the happiness of love and family—as indeed of all good things—was in a sense tied in with the realisation of socialism, which was supposed to solve all problems. Maybe *Liekki* editor Ludvig Kosonen also believed in it, although his ideas for solving the contradiction between the seriousness of class struggle and carelessness and cheerfulness of love were not optimistic ones.[48] Stories of love were very 'class-conscious'. They did not allow young workers to cross class boundaries for love's sake; love between a girl and a boy coming from different classes was seldom possible.[49] Towards the end of the decade the possibilities in this respect increased a little, and whichever of them it was belonged to the labour movement could try to convince the other of the importance of making a similar commitment.[50] On the other hand, any attempt to engage with a boy or girl of non-proletarian background was—even in love—seen as a deviation from the correct line of the class struggle.[51]

As love affairs or marriages crossing class boundaries were not common in Finland in the 1920s, this kind of story was not written in order to prevent them. The stories rather reflected a more general wish not to let the labour movement be tainted by bourgeois society. They also challenged the concept offered by love stories in other magazines, according to which it was possible for a rich man to fall in love with a poor girl and marry her.[52]

Tradition and new ideas

The short stories written by young Finnish communists in the 1920s thus ran along the lines of Finnish labour movement traditions rather than the new communist ideas. This was evident in the gloomy depictions of oppressed workers and in the moralising tones adopted towards the injustice of society. It was also traditional to portray the whole labour movement, rather than individual workers, as the hero of these stories.

Although there had been similar discussions in the Finnish labour movement as early as 1910, the criticisms of stories of workers' sufferings that were made in 1928–9, and the instructions to write about the great heroism and fighting spirit of the workers, may be seen as a reflection of the toughening attitudes of the international communist movement both towards its opponents and towards its national sections.[53] These criticisms did not actually change the character of the stories although they may have added to the number of stories recounting the strength and positive achievements of the labour movement. The lone heroes, who during the second half of the decade became more common, gained their inspiration from the tradition of Finnish working-class literature but also from the adventure stories of popular fiction and Soviet communist literature. Soviet models could perhaps gain more ground during the two last years but a communist hero dedicating himself to the cause, overcoming obstacles and inspiring others to do the same was still not typical. The strongest evidence of communist inspiration was to be found in the stories of young men giving up their private lives for the cause.

Soviet stories of dedicated heroes paid attention above all to the development of the main character, leaving the circumstances as a matter of secondary importance. The Finnish labour movement had been accustomed to the opposite and was also in the 1920s of the opinion that in a country where workers were not in power it was necessary to challenge the legitimacy of the authorities and the whole regime. Finnish communists in Finland accordingly gave these themes precedence, although the Finnish communists in the Soviet Union urged them to give more weight to the communist movement itself. They did so without great success, however, and in the course of the 1920s the attempt to turn the communists in Finland from critics and mockers to preachers was not to be achieved.

Notes

1. Jane Degras (ed.), *The Communist International 1919–1943. Documents*. Volume I 1919–1922. (London, 1956) pp.259–65.
2. On the characterisations, see e.g. 'Liebknecht-Lenin', *Itä ja Länsi*, 15 January 1925; 'Kultainen kirje', *Liekki*, 21 May 1926; 'Lenin, vallankumouksellinen nero', *Työväenjärjestöjen Tiedonantaja*, 24 January 1927.
3. Geoffrey Hosking, *Beyond Socialist Realism. Soviet fiction since Ivan Denisovich* (London, 1980) p.15; on the heroes in Soviet literature, see also Peter W. Mathewson, Jr., *The Positive Hero in Russian Literature* (Stanford, 1975) pp.167–8, 179–251; Vera S. Dunham, *In Stalin's Time. Middleclass values in Soviet fiction* (Cambridge, 1979 (1976)) pp.59–65.
4. Of the above-mentioned books the works of Gorky, London and Gladkov were translated into Finnish.
5. On the beginnings of Finnish communism, Tauno Saarela, *Suomalaisen kommunismin synty 1918–1923* (Tampere, 1996).
6. On the communist literary magazines, Tauno Saarela, 'Postilla vai Nyyrikki? Suomalainen kommunismi ja lehdet 1920-luvulla', in Jouko Joentausta (ed.), *Palstojen takaa* (Helsinki, 1997) pp.14–15; see also 'Taipaleelle', *Liekki*, 28 September 1923; on the earlier magazines, Aimo Roininen, *Kirja liikkeessä. Kirjallisuus instituutiona vanhassa työväenliikkeessä (1895–1918)* (Vammala, 1993), pp.110–15.
7. See e.g. Tatu Väätäinen, 'Raatajan palkka', *Liekki*, 5 and 12 September 1924; Antero Virta, 'tehtaan tyttö', *Liekki*, 24 October 1924; Vesa, 'Koneiden uhri', *Revontulet*, 14 October 1927; Azlag Jarga (Emil Pyttynen), '"Kuropatki"', *Liekki*, 8 and 15 August 1924; 'Yli voimien', *Revontulet*, 18 November 1927; on logging in the Finnish literature, Jyrki Pöysä, *Jätkän synty. Tutkimus sosiaalisen kategorian*

muotoutumisesta suomalaisessa kulttuurissa ja itäsuomalaisessa metsätyöperinteessä (Vammala, 1997) pp.96–8.

8. See e.g. Anna Suonio, 'Katutyttö', *Liekki*, 14 October 1927; 'Häätö', *Liekki*, 25 August 1925; Kirsti Violenti, 'Saajanlahden huutolaispoika', *Liekki*, 16 November 1923; Simson, 'Pikkurenki', *Liekki*, 25 July 1924; Alex Orjatsalo, 'Raatajan palkka', *Liekki*, 11 January 1924; Veli, 'Uhraaja', *Liekki*, 6 June 1924; Pohjanpoika, Elämän armoton todellisuus, *Liekki*, 9 April 1926.

9. Kaarlo Valli, 'Käsipuolen tarina', *Liekki*, 29 July 1927; Ossi Ahtola, 'Rahaa, rahaa—leipää, leipää', *Liekki*, 21 March 1924; Lauri Kanto, 'Luisuvalla tiellä', *Liekki*, 9 October 1925.

10. Veli, 'Eräs joulu', *Liekki*, 21 December 1923; Lauri L., 'Laulajan tarina', *Liekki*, 15 February 1924.

11. On working-class literature in Finland, Raoul Palmgren, edited by Jouko Joentausta *Työläiskirjallisuus (Proletaarikirjallisuus). Kirjallisuus- ja aatehistoriallinen käsiteselvittely* (Porvoo, 1965), pp.165–6; on Finnish realism, Päivi Lappalainen, 'Epäkohdat esiin—Realistit maailmaa parantamassa', in *Järkiuskosta vaistojen kapinaan. Suomen kirjallisuushistoria 2.* Toimittanut Lea Rojola (Helsinki, 1999), pp.11–12.

12. See e.g. Yrjö M-la, 'Mitä ja miten on *Liekki*in kirjoitettava?', *Liekki*, 23 May 1924.

13. Jeppe, 'Petiittinikkarin toilauksia', *Liekki*, 16 November 1928; 'Mitä lehdestämme sanotaan', *Liekki*, 4 January 1929.

14. Ludvig Kosonen, 'Proletaarisesta ja porvarillisesta taiteesta', *Liekki*, 2 August 1929.

15. Ludvig Kosonen, 'Ajopuita elämän virrassa', *Revontulet*, 14, 21 and 28 June, 5, 12 and 19 July 1929.

16. Ludvig Kosonen, *Lippulaulu. Kuvaus Suomen kommunistisen nuorisoaktiivin elämästä vuodelta 1929* (Leningrad, 1932).

17. See e.g. E. Salometsä, 'Siellä missä kynttilät eivät loistaneet', *Liekki*, 21 December 1928.

18. See e.g. Veli, 'Pimeiltä poluilta', *Liekki*, 26 October 1923; Tikka, 'Iltamatyttö', *Liekki*, 28 March 1924; Antero Virta, 'Eeva', *Liekki*, 24 October 1924; Hely Haihtuva, 'Lautatarhan tyttö', *Liekki*, 30 January 1925.

19. See e.g. Vennu, 'Murhaaja tuomarina', *Liekki*, 14 November 1924; Anni Koffert, 'Kenen syy?', *Liekki*, 27 March 1925.

20. 'Aaron Kepulin liikeyritys', *Liekki*, 15 February 1929.

21. Veli Luokka, 'Suunnitelma', *Liekki*, 21 December 1928 and 4 January 1929.

22. See e.g., Tikka, 'Iltamatyttö', *Liekki*, 28 March 1924; Työläissisko, 'Oikealla tiellä', *Liekki*, 4 April 1924; Usko Varma, 'Suojelija', *Liekki*, 5 December 1924.

23. Lauri Kanto, '"Yhteiskunnalle vaarallinen"', *Liekki*, 4 February 1927; on the Socialist Youth League, Nestori Parkkari, *Nuoret taistelun tiellä. Suomen vallankumouksellinen nuorisoliike 1900–1944* (Kuopio, 1970), pp.132–6.

24. M.R.Y. (Armas Äikiä), 'Pommi- ja dynamiittiliitto', *Liekki*, 24 June 1926; see also Maailmanrannan ylioppilas (Armas Äikiä), 'Suuri salaliitto', *Itä ja Länsi*, 30 November 1925.

25. Pekka Päävahti (Ludvig Kosonen), 'Suurenmoinen paljastus kommunistien

aseellisesta toiminnasta', *Liekki,* 10 May 1929; see also Kaarlo Valli, 'Ladatun helvetinkoneen hirveä salaisuus', *Liekki,* 1, 8 and 15 March 1929.

26. Tikka, 'Iltamatyttö', *Liekki,* 28 March 1924; Tikka, 'Veeran viha', *Liekki,* 6 June 1924; Inga, 'Nuoren taistelijan kokemus', *Liekki,* 29 August 1924; -o, 'Lailan särkyneet unelmat', *Liekki,* 10 July 1925.
27. See e.g. Hellä Kotijärvi, 'Elämän ulapalla', *Liekki,* 7, 14, 21 and 28 March, 4, 11, 18 and 25 April 1924; Maiju, 'Hotellin tiskityttö', *Liekki* 25 February 1927; Iikka Kare (Otto Oinonen), 'Erään tytön muistikirjasta', *Liekki,* 30 September, 7, 14, 21 and 28 October, 4, 11, 18 and 25 November, 2, 9 and 16 December 1927.
28. Ossi Ahtola, 'Rahaa, rahaa—leipää, leipää', *Liekki,* 21 March 1924; Maailmanrannan ylioppilas (Armas Äikiä), 'Työmies Rissasen loppu', *Liekki,* 21 August 1925.
29. A. Eronen, 'Työlakko', *Liekki,* 11 September 1925.
30. Kaarlo Valli, 'Leipää—oikeutta', *Liekki,* 30 September 1927; A.E., 'Taistelu leivästä', *Liekki,* 10 February 1928; Taistelijatar, 'Kaksi tunnelmaa', *Liekki,* 19 October 1928, A. O-lo, 'Joko—tahi', *Liekki,* 3 May 1929.
31. Pirjo Ala-Kapee-Marjaana Valkonen, *Yhdessä elämä turvalliseksi. SAK: laisen ammattiyhdistysliikkeen kehitys vuoteen 1930* (Helsinki, 1982) pp.718–29.
32. Iikka Kare (Otto Oinonen), 'Kumpusaaren kesävieraat', *Liekki,* 20 July 1928.
33. Kalle Rissanen, 'Solu', *Liekki,* 17 and 24 September, 1, 8, 15, 22 and 29 October, 5, 12 and 19 November 1926.
34. Palmgren, *Työläiskirjallisuus,* p.151.
35. See e.g. Kaarlo Valli, 'Viimeiset laukaukset', *Liekki,* 3 September 1926; Kaarlo Valli, 'Yksi monista', *Liekki,* 22 July 1927.
36. See e.g. K. K-o, 'Yhdennellätoista hetkellä', *Liekki,* 25 April 1924; Are L-n, 'Kotitarkastus', *Revontulet,* 10 September 1926; Aatto Lahtio, 'Takaa-ajettuna', *Revontulet,* 8 October 1926; Risto Karu, 'Marusja', *Revontulet,* 23 September 1927; Maailmanrannan ylioppilas (Armas Äikiä), 'San Juan alkuasukaskommunisti', *Liekki,* 21 January 1927.
37. See e.g. Henriks D:son (Kyösti Kivi), 'Työläisluokan nuoriso ja laiskuriluokan ajanvietekirjallisuus', *Liekki,* 5 June 1925.
38. K. Brown-Wolf (Kyösti Kivi), 'Varastettu valtionhoitaja', *Liekki,* 22 and 29 January, 5, 12 and 19 February 1926.
39. On this kind of popular fiction, see e.g. Timo Kukkola, *Hornanlinnan perilliset. 70 vuotta suomalaista salapoliisikirjallisuutta* (Porvoo, 1980) pp.64, 78–80.
40. 'Kapinaromantiikkaa', *Itä ja Länsi,* 15 October 1924.
41. Azlag Jarga, '"Humu"', *Liekki,* 4 March 1927.
42. Armas Äikiä, 'Apusahuri', in *Työläiskynäilijäin ja kuvaajain liitto Yhteisvoiman albumi I* (Helsinki, 1929), pp.29–33.
43. Eino Kataja, Olavi Borglund, *Liekki,* 15 June 1928.
44. See e.g. Mildred Cram, 'Musta silkkinuora', *Revontulet,* 19 and 26 November, 3 December 1926; 'Rakkaustarina Etelämeren saarilta', *Revontulet,* 31 December 1926; Stacy Aumonier, 'Rakkaus vaiko kuningaskunta', *Revontulet,* 6 and 13 May 1927; 'Ruhtinattaren lemmentarina', *Revontulet,* 8 July 1927; 'Filminäyttelijättären

rakkaus', *Revontulet*, 10 August 1928.
45. Usko Varma, 'Onnen kukkanen', *Liekki*, 22 December 1924.
46. Veli, 'Voimakkaita tunteita', *Liekki*,15 February 1924; I.N., 'Saavuttamisen arvoinen ystävyys', *Liekki*, 20 February 1925; Tikka, 'Toveruus ja rakkaus', *Liekki*, 6 March 1925; Anna Suonio, '"Anna minun olla toverisi"', *Liekki*, 2 March 1928.
47. Iita Nuotio, 'Kukkivien tuomien alla', *Liekki*, Midsummer 1925; Kyynelten lemmikki, 'Mökin Johanna', *Liekki*, 30 April 1926; Marit Matkakoski, 'Tyttö potkukelkassa', *Revontulet*, 4 November 1927.
48. Ludvig Kosonen, 'Ajopuita elämän virrassa', *Revontulet*, 14, 21 and 28 June, 5, 12 and 19 July 1928.
49. See e.g. Azlag Jarga, 'Kaksi ihmistä', *Liekki*, 2 and 9 May 1924; Ida Hagert, 'Aatteen vuoksi', *Liekki*, 15 August 1924; Hemmi Aro, 'Oman luokkansa lapsia', *Liekki*, 10 October 1924; Aarne Linnansaari, Nukkuva kaupunki, *Revontulet*, 16 April 1926.
50. See e.g. Anna Suonio, 'Paulan taistelu', *Liekki*, 22 July 1928; E.L. Suksi, 'Sosialistipuhuja', *Liekki*, 24 May 1929.
51. Iikka Kare, 'Takaisin maankamaralle', *Liekki*, 22 and 29 June, 3 July and 3 August 1928; Taistelijatar, 'Uskollinen vakaumukselleen', *Liekki*, 31 August 1928; Risto Karu, '"Muista kuka olet!"', *Liekki*, 19 October 1928.
52. On the love stories, Ulla Eloranta, '"Villiorvokkien huuma". Naistenviihde populaarikulttuurin kentässä', in *Aika on aikaa...Tutkielma poploresta*. Toimittanut Seppo Knuuttila (Helsinki, 1975), pp.166–8.
53. On the earlier discussion, Aimo Roininen, 'Työväenliike tuo työläiset kirjallisuuden kentille', in *Järkiuskosta*, p.101.

A Party Blocked
West German communists between Weimar legacy and East German policy, 1945–1956

Till Kössler

Emerging from the Second World War as a major political force with substantial support in the population, by the mid-1950s the Communist Party of Germany (KPD) had lost most of its following and influence. Recent scholarship has stressed the role of the West German 'economic miracle', the persecution of the party by federal and state authorities and errors of judgement by the communist party leadership in this process.[1] Although these points were certainly of importance, I want to argue that internal conflicts within the party, reflecting broader generational and political rifts within the postwar German working-class, were a major reason for the decline of the KPD. The division of Germany in particular weighed heavily on the party.

For many years, the history of the KPD has been written primarily from a top-down perspective. The interaction between the different factions of the party elite and the relationship of the German party with the CPSU and the Comintern have been the main points of study. Only recently has new scholarly work emerged stressing the importance of studying the social basis of the party, the rank and file and the local milieux in which they lived, arguing that only through such a change of perspective can a richer understanding of party development be obtained.[2]

In examining the interaction between party elite and party membership in the West German KPD in the postwar era, I want to take a middle ground between these two positions. My starting point is the observation that the KPD was by no means as monolithic as it portrayed itself in public statements and as it was presented by its political opponents. Rather, it was Janus-like. One face showed a centralised and hierarchical party organisation under the leadership of the East German ruling party, the Socialist Unity Party (SED). The other, less visible face, revealed a party that struggled hard to integrate party factions with very different political traditions and generational outlooks. Moreover, it had to reconcile the party orders of the East German leadership with the interests of the West German rank and file rooted in a particular political generation and social milieu which preserved the party traditions and culture of the 1920s.

My argument is that the decline of communism in West Germany after 1945 was in large part the result of a conflict between the increasingly East German-dominated party organisation and its demands on the individual member on the one hand, and the West German party milieu with its traditional value system on the other. Although the conflict between the different concepts of what the party's priorities should be was never fought out in public, the internal struggle dominated party affairs in the late 1940s and early 1950s to such an extent that it intensified existing conflicts and political tensions within the membership and eventually proved self destructive to the party. While a core of communists, mostly party veterans, moved closer together and cut themselves off from broader political developments, the majority of members who had joined in the immediate postwar years slowly detached themselves from the party.

In order to show how this internal conflict over goals divided and ultimately destroyed the party in West Germany, the article is divided into four sections. In the first section I look at the composition, development and cohesion of the party membership after 1945. The second section shows the diversity of political outlooks in the KPD in the first postwar years, which the party leadership found it hard to integrate, and explores the tensions between the faction of long-time communists on the one hand and the communists who joined the party just after 1945 on the other. The third section describes in some detail the efforts by the East German SED to integrate the party behind its political agenda from the late 1940s and the prominent role the concept of the 'cadre party' played in this regard. Finally, the fourth section offers some observations on the effectiveness or otherwise of efforts by the party leadership to gain acceptance for its policy and discipline the party membership.

Old cadres and new members

Most contemporary observers and the majority of historical researchers have taken the communists' self-image of a tightly knit 'cadre-party' at face value. This interpretation perseveres, moreover, because, rather like the party itself, the political opponents of the KPD portrayed the communists as fanatic and loyal followers of Stalin and Walter Ulbricht, the political leader of the emerging East German state. I do not want to argue here that this wide-spread image did not describe an important part of the communist party culture. But a closer look at the communist locals shows that the KPD emerged after 1945 as a highly heterogeneous party. Two groups of communists in particular can be distinguished, each with its own political agenda and outlook. On the one hand, there were 'old communists' who had entered the party before 1933 and had to a great extent internalised the party culture of the 1920s. They formed specific local communist milieux with their own value system and way of life. On the other hand, workers without a party political background and with no intimate knowledge of the Weimar KPD entered the KPD in great numbers after 1945. They wanted to participate in the rebuilding of Germany and felt that after the collapse of National Socialism, communism offered the only way out of the present misery.

The national socialist movement had tried completely to destroy the communist party and its subculture. During the twelve years of Nazi rule, the KPD had suffered enormous losses both of members and party officials through Nazi terror.[3] Moreover, many communist exiles in the Soviet Union were killed in the Stalinist purges of the 1930s.[4] In the immediate postwar years, however, the KPD was again able to attract a substantial following in a surprisingly short time. Party membership in the three western zones quickly rose after 1945, to reach 300,000 by the spring of 1947. In most places, the KPD significantly increased its membership to above the highest prewar level.[5] The KPD was thus not only a veterans' party of Weimar communism, but also a party with a distinctively postwar outlook.

It is true that long-time party members formed the backbone of the postwar KPD and dominated party life. In 1949, a third of all members were old cadres who had joined the communist movement before 1933. Although National Socialism was partly successful in destroying the communist subculture, it thus reemerged, albeit reduced in scale, after the Second World War. Almost everywhere, after the liberation by the allied armies, former members of the KPD started immediately to rebuild local party organisations. Sometimes even membership fees for the past twelve years were collected to demonstrate symbolically the continuity of the party over the dark years of National Socialist rule. This group of communists was characterised by a high degree of social, generational, and political cohesion. First of all, almost all of them came from working-class families. In 1954, industrial workers and their families accounted for more than 85 per cent of the membership. The KPD was especially strong in the metal, mining and shipbuilding trades. In a party convention of the Ruhr district in 1946, for example, two-thirds of the delegates were miners and steelworkers by profession.[6]

Moreover, the 'old communists' formed a special generational unit. Mostly born between 1895 and 1910, they joined the organised labour movement in their teens, entered the KPD in the 1920s and consciously lived through the world economic crisis of the early 1930s and the destruction of the Weimar Republic. During the National Socialist era, they mostly kept together in informal circles of friends, after their initial sacrificial revolt against the National Socialist state proved futile. This generational group of communists grew up politically in the militant party culture of the 1920s and internalised its world-view and value system. It developed a communist lifestyle which survived to a surprising extent the political changes of 1933 and 1945 and still dominated party life in the 1950s.[7]

The make-up of the female membership of the KPD underlines its character as a milieu party. The membership had a clear male bias. The KPD was predominantly a party of working-class men. Female communists accounted for just 15 to 20 per cent of the membership although women were overrepresented due to war losses. Being for the most part born in the decades before and after 1900, their generational makeup represented that of their male counterparts. The male dominance in the party does not conflict with the observation that the communist milieu was structured and reinforced by family ties. Wives and daughters of communist activists constituted the largest part of the female membership. While 82 per cent of the female communists worked as housewives, only a small minority were wage earners.[8] In most communist strongholds, there existed communist dynasties, stretching over three or more generations. Police reports of the 1950s, for example, frequently mentioned the fact that communist agitators came from 'old communist families'.[9]

These family ties were the most important reason for the ability of the KPD to attract a segment of the working-class youth after the war. Through the families, communist values and traditions were handed down to a younger generation who grew up as '*Kriegskinder*' (children of the war) during the early 1940s and constituted the bulk of the members of the *Freie Deutsche Jugend* (Free German Youth), the party youth organisation. As the sons and daughters of communist parents, the young communists were themselves an integral part of the communist milieux.[10]

Communist families stood at the centre of local communist milieux which reemerged in most industrial cities after 1945. Although most of its Weimar Republic strongholds had eroded to a certain extent, there still existed until the mid-1950s communist communities in certain quarters of larger industrial cities like Hamburg, Essen and Düsseldorf. These 'little Moscows' were often situated in the vicinity of large plants or pits. In the city of Hattingen in the Ruhr valley, for example, there still existed a neighbourhood in 1953 in which 'there are only communist families. All men are members of the KPD'.[11] The communist milieux were clearly eroded during the 1950s, but a hard core survived the banning of the KPD in 1956. In 'years of joint work stretching over decades', as a report put it in 1959, the communists themselves had become a 'loyal family'.[12]

But while, on the one hand, the generational and milieu-based character of the KPD was the prerequisite for the quick reestablishment of the KPD as a mass party after 1945, on the other hand it hindered the lasting expansion of the party beyond its core following. The communist party had extreme problems after 1945 in recruiting members of younger generations or people from non-working class backgrounds. Even the above-mentioned *Kriegskinder* generation only accounted for a small part of the membership. In particular, the KPD was never really successful in recruiting a considerable number of members of the so-called 'Hitler youth' generation, born in the early- and middle-1920s and educated under the Nazi regime in the 1930s. In 1954, therefore, almost half the membership in West Germany was older than 50 years, whereas only 6 per cent of the members were younger than 25 years of age. Between 1951 and 1953 alone, the percentage of members above the age of 50 increased by thirteen per cent.[13]

The milieu-based limitations of West German communism becomes especially apparent if one looks at the party members who only entered the party after 1945. Distinguished by high prestige after the defeat of National Socialism because of its uncompromising opposition to Nazi rule, the KPD was able to recruit thousands of new activists from among the working classes in the immediate postwar years who had only little knowledge of communist traditions. In the late 1940s, two-thirds of the entire membership had entered the party after 1945, leaving the 'old communists' in a minority position. The new supporters of the KPD had for the most part a similiar social background to that of the old comrades. They belonged to the middle-aged, male industrial workforce which had lived through the final years of the Weimar Republic and experienced National Socialism, at least in its final years, as an oppressive and exploiting regime. But although the majority of the new members belonged to the same social and generational cohort as the old members and shared the experience of industrial labour, there existed marked differences in political values and outlook between them. As will be shown below, the new members as a whole never really integrated into communist party culture. However, before turning to the disputes within the rank and file, it is necessary to take a closer look at the interaction between the party leadership and the communist locals.

The struggle for political orientation

Although the KPD again developed into a major political force, its political unity and stability was fragile from the beginning. After twelve years of

National Socialist rule, during which contact between the party elites and the communist locals had mostly been cut off, there existed strikingly different concepts of what the character of communist politics should be. For most of the old members, National Socialism had not only meant a period of extreme persecution, but also one of defeat and traumatisation. The high hopes of the early 1930s when the victory of socialism seemed to be within reach had turned into frustration and, often, despair when the communists realised that Hitler found overwhelming support within German society.[14] The political pressure on the communists resulted in an even closer adherence to the traditions and culture of the party. A strong emphasis on class struggle, revolution and workers' rights especially perservered through the years of Nazi rule. It is no surprise therefore, that most of the communist locals which started to rebuild the party in 1945 wanted 'to pick up work right there where they have left it in 1933'.[15] The delegates to the first party conference in the Ruhr area who still wanted to fight for 'Soviet-Germany' represented the overwhelming majority of the surviving members.[16]

Contrary to the 1920s, however, this 'revolutionary' political agenda clashed with the new prerogatives of the party leadership. Influenced by the failure to prevent Hitler's rise to power and pressured by the Comintern, the exiled party elites in Moscow had drastically changed the party line in order to attract a mass following after the end of the war.[17] Instead of radical socialist goals, the party in its programmatic statement on 11 June 1945 outlined a more moderate policy and called for a broad coalition of all antifascists. The socialisation of industries, for example, was hardly mentioned. To make itself acceptable as a partner to other political forces, the KPD also rid itself of its former rhetoric of class struggle and instead used a language of national duty and unity.[18]

The political shift of the party leadership as it manifested itself in countless public proclamations and party orders took most of the party veterans by surprise. During the time of National Socialist rule only sparse information about the new 'popular front' direction of the party, which stressed the national responsibility of the KPD, had trickled into Germany. Therefore, it is not surprising that during the summer of 1945 numerous reports reached the party headquarters in East Berlin informing the leadership about a lack of understanding and even outright resistance in the membership when faced with the new political agenda. Even the high ranking officals of the provisional Ruhr district leadership had to confess in the summer of 1945 'that it did not wholly understand the new direction of the party'.[19]

In spite of the irritation and opposition of the rank and file communist party milieu, the leadership was able to make the new popular front agenda binding within a surprisingly short time. Already in early August 1945, for example, the Ruhr district leadership proudly reported to East Berlin, that 'the political reorientation was executed without hesitation'.[20] Although the report kept quiet about the convincing it took to bring the membership in line, nonetheless its basic message is correct. The always well-informed observers of the British military government in Germany, for example, similarly reported during the second half of 1945 that 'the party as a whole follows the Berlin line'.[21]

What were the reasons for this voluntary submission of the communist locals to the party leadership without any major conflict? First, the party culture of the KPD has to be taken into account. The reason for the obedience of the rank and file can be traced back less to the persuasive power of the new arguments than to the party discipline which was such an important feature of communist party culture. The communists saw themselves as part of a tightly knit, disciplined and hierarchically structured 'cadre party'. At the base of this party concept, which can only be outlined roughly here, lay a strictly dichotomous world-view and the conviction that under the existing social and political conditions a socialist revolution could only be successful if it were prepared by a centralised and disciplined vanguard party. For the communists, politics was a fundamental struggle between the forces of progress and the forces of reaction which could not be solved by compromise. The party saw itself as the driving force of progress and as teacher of the broader working class. It was communist faith that the political development was steered by fundamental historical laws. This faith served as the basis for the hierarchical construction of the party organisation. Only the communist leadership, with a strong communist conviction, acquired through long years of study and practical experience, was capable of determining the right course for the party. Internal democracy was therefore extremely limited.

All in all, the party was modelled along military lines. While it was the leadership's task and privilege to work out the strategy and 'party line', the membership had to attend and execute detailed orders. Like a military unit, the party followers had unquestioningly to carry out whatever commands they received from the leadership. The KPD, moreover, laid claim to the whole person of its followers. Commitment to the party had to be total. Already when entering the organisation, the individual member had to declare 'to fight untiring for the realisation of the party resolutions [...] and be a constant agitator for the cause of the party'.[22] The widespread use of military vocabulary in the party underscores this proximity to the world of the military.

The communist self-image, as roughly sketched above, not only shaped the thinking of the party elite, the paid officials at the federal and district level, but extended far into the rank and file. The party executive of the Ruhr district wrote to party headquarters in Berlin, for example, that when faced with party directives the communist locals showed an 'extraordinary good discipline'.[23] In later years, too, the internal party correspondence frequently mentioned the loyalty of the membership. The vocabulary of unity and dicipline was not only lofty rhetoric, but an essential element of the political life of most communists. After the workers' revolt in the GDR on 17 June 1953, for example, the greater part of the KPD membership kept 'strict discipline' in spite of serious doubts about the situation in the East. The experience of persecution between 1933 and 1945 had reinforced the stress the communists put on party discipline. It had become communist conviction that only through strict adherence to party orders and unity could the party be succesful.[24] For most convinced communists the party was an ersatz family to which they were bound not just by political reasoning, but also by close emotional ties. These ties made prolonged opposition to party directives emotionally and politically extremely difficult.

The high prestige of the party leadership in East Berlin was a second reason for the voluntary submission of the rank and file in the western zones. All former high-ranking party leaders of Weimar communism had taken residence in East Berlin while the district executives in the West were almost entirely former middle or lower strata party officials. For the communists, it was therefore quite natural to follow the lead of East Berlin.

Thirdly, the historical circumstances have to be kept in mind. The task of rebuilding the party under conditions of destruction and want demanded much attention from the communist locals. Rebuilding work often left them little time to consider what many of them felt were merely theoretical debates detached from day-to-day party affairs. Moreover, many communists saw in the political about-turn only a tactical move to win over the German people to communism.[25]

Finally, there existed doubts among the West German communists, too, as to whether the old concepts and methods of class struggle were adequate for the new historical situation. Even before news of the popular front policy reached the Ruhr early in the summer of 1945, a heated debate about the future course of the party had been going on within the provisional district leadership. Although most members wanted to continue politics unchanged along the lines of the Weimar party, others argued for a thorough stocktaking of communist politics after the fall of National Socialism.[26] To some extent, these debates anticipated the arguments by the party hierarchy and prepared the ground for the acceptance of the new party line.

It is true that, as described above, in 1945 the party executive under Wilhelm Pieck and Walter Ulbricht was successful in making the new party line of popular front reconciliation binding within the party. However, that does not dismiss the fact that strong reservations against the new policy remained within the party. The alliance between the leadership and the local party organisations was fragile right from the start. In 1945, the party elites achieved only superficial consent within the rank and file. As the following paragraphs will show, there existed starkly differing opinions among the members as what the party's goals should be. These differences can be traced back to the social make-up of the party. The new members especially, those who were not rooted in the party tradition, supported a moderate policy. The older communists favoured a more radical and uncompromising political approach. Both positions, however, only partially complied with the party line.

Already in the summer of 1945, differences between the older, more radical communists and a politically more pragmatic faction which mainly comprised the new element in the party became visible. Among the party veterans there existed a marked ressentment against the new members. They often voiced the conviction that 'the old comrades are the most reliable; the new members [...] who entered the party in 1945 are of no use'.[27] In many places, the old communists kept to themselves 'being content for the moment to have grouped together again'.[28]

The internal differences were especially pronounced over the question of how far the party should ally itself to the Soviet Union. In an environment of virulent anti-Russian sentiment, the communists were frequently forced to define their position towards the Soviet occupation force. While there existed strong pro-Soviet sympathies in the traditional communist milieu, many new communists tried to distance the party as far as possible from the Bolshevik state. In many regions, an 'enthusiasm for Russia, the Red Army, and Russian methods' could be found alomgside attempts by members 'to dissociate themselves from Russian communism'.[29] In the Hannover region, for example, the KPD was 'almost anti-Russian in sentiment' and followed a 'very moderate policy'.[30] At the end of 1946, the British military government did not even discount the possibility that an anti-Russian faction would split off from the KPD and set up a new communist party independent from Moscow.[31]

There were similar tensions within the communist membership regarding the demand by the party leadership to seek cooperation with the Social Democrats and form a 'united front' of the working-class parties. While, on the one hand, there are many examples of a good understanding between the parties at a local level, many communists distrusted the SPD and wanted to keep to themselves politically. The Ruhr district executive, for example, noted in the summer of 1945 that regarding the Social Democrats 'there are frequent signs of the old politics of 1930–1933' within the membership—the time, that is, when the KPD bitterly fought the SPD under the battle-cry of 'social fascism'.[32] Even among the middle-ranking party officials, there existed such a marked dislike of German social democracy that the zonal executive for the British zone had constantly to remind them 'not to take up a stance of total opposition' against the SPD.[33]

The tensions between radical and moderate party factions also expressed themselves in the debate about the character of the KPD in postwar Germany. On the one hand, the moderate wing appropriated the demand of the party leadership to model the KPD into a 'true people's party' with mass appeal.[34] Members of the Cologne district, for example, demanded that the party should no longer define itself as a political elite.[35] On the other hand, most of the old communists opposed an 'unhealthy growth through a mass recruitment of members', arguing that this would damage the strength of the KPD. They rather wanted to keep to themselves and favoured a 'small, but powerful' party.[36]

For the most part, the boundaries between the two camps within the KPD remained fluid. However, it regularly happened that internal conflicts led to open clashes between the two factions at local level. From the Bremen district, for example, in 1947 the British consulate reported 'marked tensions between the old time revolutionaries and those who favoured more subtle methods'.[37] In the Westphalian city of Münster, a large proportion of the membership even split off from the KPD after a prolonged period of inner-party dispute, complaining about undemocratic methods within the party. The British military government expected the renegades to eventually join the SPD.[38]

Internal strife was not limited to the KPD, but is a feature of almost every political organisation. In the KPD, however, the internal tensions were particularly difficult to reconcile as they expressed starkly different political outlooks. Moreover, the party did not possess procedures to defuse internal dispute, but, on the contrary, the strong emphasis it put on discipline and unity made it difficult to voice opposition within the party. Finally, the party leadership reinforced the conflict through its policy of pushing through its political agenda at all costs.

The political heterogeneity within the rank and file posed a major problem for the party leadership in East Berlin because it threatened to undermine its authority and power over the party organisation in the West. In the following section, I will further elaborate this point and describe the strategies of the party executive to integrate the party behind it and to secure its power in the western zones.

Disciplining the KPD

The history of communism in West Germany after 1945 cannot be written without taking into account the division of Germany and the German question. Soon after the occupation of Germany, the KPD found itself in an awkward position. In the Eastern zone, it slowly emerged, with the substantial help of the Soviet military government's suppression of oppositional political forces, as the ruling party in a Soviet satellite state. In the three western zones, by contrast, the party became a political outsider and outcast.

The development of two different states with divergent political cultures on German territory after 1945 created a fundamental problem for the KPD which continued to define itself as part of a trans-German party. The interests of the communists in the West increasingly differed from the interests of the communist leadership in the East. While the former called for a pan-German perspective of communist politics, the latter accorded absolute priority to the securing of power in its sphere of influence and support for Soviet policy towards Germany, not support for the party in the western zones.[39]

The Socialist Unity Party (SED) policy towards the KPD was dominated by the objective of modelling the KPD into a propaganda tool for its policy in the West. The party headquarters tried through various measures to subjugate to its goals the communist locals in the West, to stamp out dissenting positions there, and to curb any attempts by the West German communists to achieve a greater degree of independence. In these objectives, the SED leadership faced the problem that it could not exert direct control over its followers in the western zones, but had to rely on the party hierarchy there to transmit its directives. Therefore, to reach and maintain a tight grip on the party organisation was of foremost importance to the party leaders. The problem of control became especially acute when the division of Germany and the creation of an executive office for West Germany separated the SED headquarters even more from the West German organisation and made communication within the party more difficult.

The West German KPD remained during the whole time of its existence an integral part of the SED.[40] The different development in the single zones and the difficulty of maintaining close communication between the zones, however, provoked demands for an organisational adaptation to the new political situation. In particular the merger of the KPD with the Social Democratic Party (SPD) in the Eastern zone in April 1946, which made the

KPD an awkward appendix to the new Socialist Unity Party (SED), fuelled the debate about an organisational restructuring in the West. In the summer of 1946, West German party officials continuously complained that West German matters were not taken seriously by the East German headquarters. In their opinion, it was all but impossible to coordinate politics in the West under the present circumstances. In 1946 there were even proposals by officials in the West to set up their own headquarters for the western zones. Many communists felt that more elbow room for the West German organisation was necessary if the party were to remain a political force in the western zones.[41] The high-ranking party secretary Walter Fisch from Hessia, for example, held that 'the completely different situation in the West' demanded a 'seperate political approach towards all everyday matters'.[42]

Without explicitly rejecting these demands, the party leadership never gave in to them. On the contrary, they tried to make the organisation better suited to their needs. After experimenting with different forms of intermediate institutions between the party headquarters and the western districts, a party executive office for West Germany was finally installed in March 1948. This move, however, was more a response to the changing political environment after the beginning of the Cold War than to the demands of the western districts. The formal independence of the West German KPD meant neither an organisational nor a political break from the SED. Quite the reverse, the political subordination of the West German KPD under the SED increased after 1948.[43] Wilhelm Pieck, one of the most powerful communist leaders in the eastern zone, thus demanded that the 'internal links to the KPD should not be broken off [...] but, on the contrary, further be strengthened'.[44] To this effect, the SED leadership established so-called west sections in the central committee, at the district level and in all major 'mass organisations' which had the task to instruct and supervise the western party organisation.[45] The leadership of the KPD in the West had merely executive responsibilities and only limited self-governing power.

In the late 1940s, two developments combined to increase the pressure on the KPD in the West. First, the party in this period was in decline. While it could still muster substantial support in the first elections after the war, especially in the urban and industrial regions, from 1948 onwards its voting figures quickly dropped. In the federal elections of 1949, the party only just cleared the 5 per cent hurdle (5.7 per cent of all votes cast) needed to enter the new federal parliament, the Bundestag. Four years later, in 1953, the party finally lost its Bundestag seats since just 2.2 per cent of all voters cast their ballot for the Communist Party. In addition, membership figures dropped drastically and between 1947 and 1951, the KPD lost more than half of its members.⁴⁶ This development was highly unsatisfactory both to the West German communists and the East Berlin leadership. Although its East-centred policy was a major reason for the failure of the KPD, party headquarters put the whole blame for the situation in the West on the party organisation. In an 'objectively' favourable historical situation 'ideological and organisational weakness' were made responsible for the bad showing of the KPD in the elections.⁴⁷

The second development, coinciding with the decline of the KPD, was the outbreak of the Cold War and commencement in 1949 of an ideological offensive in the West by the SED. After the establishment of the Federal Republic and the GDR, the East German leadership made a major effort to win over the West German population and at the same time legitimise its rule in the East.⁴⁸ The KPD was a major weapon in this war of propaganda. Therefore, control over the West German party became especially urgent for the SED leadership.

The heavy interventions of the SED into the KPD's party affairs took place within this political setting. The SED tried on a number of levels to gain complete control over the communist locals in the West. Most far-reaching was the enormous expansion of the already existing 'instructor' apparatus. The SED, the East German 'mass organisations' and to a lesser extent the West German party executives, employed instructors who transmitted the party line to the rank and file, supervised the execution of orders and reported the outcome back to the party. The instructors were allowed to interfere in local party matters and to give orders to the local activists. Through the use of instructors, the party executive hoped directly to influence the shape of Communist politics in the West. The party headquarters demanded that the instructors 'should secure the leadership of the party executive in the western zones'.⁴⁹

Furthermore, the party leaders expanded the system of political instruction within the party to root out deviating views which were defamed as 'ideological weaknesses'. Already in the summer of 1945, the Ruhr district leadership declared that 'political instruction along the lines laid out by the central committee' was 'the most important task' of the future.⁵⁰ Gradually over the post-war years, political instruction was intensified. Party schools were set up in the western zones as well as in the East and at the local level the party made participation in weekly instruction evenings mandatory.⁵¹

Another measure to keep control over the organisation was direct interference in the personal structure of the lower levels of the party hierarchy. In the Essen district, for example, the party executive replaced 22 party secretaries between March 1951 and May 1952, even though the district leadership had been elected just a few months before, in January 1951. The first secretary of the district alone was replaced four times.[52] These interventions had the objective of preventing the formation of local centres of power that potentially weakened the influence of the party elite on the individual member. In 1951, the party explicitly demanded and pushed through the 'removal of district kings' who had implicitly challenged the authority of the national leadership and were criticised for their alleged self-satisfied manners.[53] The East Berlin headquarters routinely replaced the older 'party fathers' with young communists who were well trained in Marxist-Leninist ideology but lacked the experience of party work at the local level. Moreover, the young cadres mostly were not familiar with the local party organisations they had to work in. Nevertheless, they were loyal to the party line.

The most visible measure used to discipline the communist locals in the West was outright expulsion. Especially between 1949 and 1952 a number of purges took place, removing real or alleged deviators from office and often expelling them from the party.[54] Although the party did not have such extensive disciplinary power in the West as in its own sphere of power, the mere threat of expulsion had a disciplinary effect for most party members.

The examples illustrate the constant interventions into the structure and work of the party by the leadership. Through its disciplinary policy, the leadership was able to prevent the emergence of local centres of power which could in the long run have threatened the position of the party elite. Moreover the examples show that the exercise of power by the SED/KPD executive adhered to the dominant technocratic model of party politics. The SED/KPD leaders held loyalty and an abstract theoretical knowledge of class struggle as the key virtues which lower level party functionaries needed to possess. In contrast, intimate knowledge of local traditions and conditions was of little importance.

Limitations of the cadre party

The milieu character of the KPD in the different towns and regions of West Germany had direct implications for the politics of the party. It was the main reason for the inner-party resistance against the directives from East Berlin which became a central feature of the KPD development in the late 1940s and 1950s. The existence of a communist milieu with a specific tradition, value system and a distinguishable way of life prevented the thorough implementation of a top-down party structure. The rank-and-file communists increasingly refused to execute the party line. In most cases, the tensions between the demands of the cadre party and milieu-orientation within the organisation did not result in open conflicts. The stress that the communist discourse put on discipline and unity in the face of party orders prevented an open articulation of discontent. Instead, dissatisfaction with the politics and the development of the KPD articulated itself in widespread disobedience to the party line and a silent refusal to obey the diverse orders of the executive which could be reconciled less and less with the world-view and values of the rank and file.

In the first postwar years the tensions within the party were concealed by the demands of organisational rebuilding and the common hope that a socialist future lay around the corner. From 1948 onwards, however, in a situation of Cold War polarisation the internal rifts increasingly dominated party life. It became more and more obvious that the self-image of a unified and efficient party machinery was more illusion than reality. There was a marked increase in complaints by high officials that the resolutions of the executive did not find observance beyond the ranks of the salaried employees. Often, these officials remarked that the rank and file ignored them outright.[55]

In some party locals, there even developed marked resentment against the party hierarchy. The participants in a debate in the party local in Schwenningen, a small town in Wuerttemberg, for example, charged that the party executives were the 'handymen of [federal chancellor] Adenauer who want to break up the party from the top down' and destroy the reputation of the KPD.[56] They also accused the leadership of having lost contact with the rank and file and of behaving arrogantly. To be sure, these accusations marked an extreme position. Nonetheless they represented a broad current of discontent within the rank and file. A district party secretary even estimated that 'if we threw out all members who voiced dissatisfaction with the party line, we would be left with just a few comrades, perhaps only with 10 per cent'.[57]

The opposition against the party directives was widespread, but it was not total and centred around certain issues. As the following examples show, the rank and file especially refused to execute those party orders that did not concur with traditional communist beliefs. In the first place, the resistance directed itself against the so-called national policy of the SED/KPD. In order to attract the support of former Nazi-followers, after 1945, the communist leadership used nationalistic rhetoric and promoted 'German independence'.[58] However, the party executive never succeeded in mobilising more than a small minority of the membership for its national campaign. Max Reimann, the party leader of the KPD, for example, detected in 1949 a widespread aversion among Communists to the term 'fatherland' and the federal black, red and gold colours which the party tried to promote.[59] To the dismay of the East Berlin headquarters, even high-ranking party officials did not wholly understand and propagate the national policy of the SED.[60]

In addition to the national issue, the party hierarchy's uncritical support for the GDR and the Soviet Union became a major subject of criticism. It is true that in general the majority of the rank and file idealised the Soviet Union and the 'building of Socialism' in East Germany. But even the hard core of the West German communists became increasingly critical of 'real-existing' socialist development in the GDR which, in its perception, deviated from the true path to socialism. A commonly held opinion among communists in Hamburg was: 'Before we can defend her, the GDR first has to achieve some of its self-proclaimed goals.'[61] At the core of the charges levelled against the East German leadership was the belief that the SED was betraying the cherished objectives of communism. West German KPD members frequently accused the SED of no longer being a true Marxist party, of losing contact with the working class, of giving party secretaries too many privileges and of having introduced a personality cult into the party. Moreover, the rearmament of the GDR was criticised and concerns voiced about whether 'the interests of the working people were secured in the armed forces of the GDR' and whether there were enough safeguards against the reentry of the reactionary forces.[62]

The measures by the party elites to discipline the party not only led to conflicts between leadership and rank and file but also aggravated and reinforced the tensions between the different factions of the party. In particular, the personnel policy of the party executive caused internal conflicts within the party that often took the form of generational disputes. As mentioned above, in the early 1950s the party leaders exchanged in substantial numbers older functionaries for younger cadres who were loyal to the new party line and dependent on the leadership for their party positions. These young secretaries found it almost impossible to gain the full confidence of their local, older constituency, who had known each other for years. Many 'old communists' mistrusted the younger members who had for the most part been educated in the Hitler Youth and had been open to fascist ideas. For the old comrades, they were 'contaminated by fascism and militarism', although the majority had converted to communism directly at the end of the war.[63] The tensions frequently developed into an open fight for the leadership of the local party organisation and diverted energies from regular political activities. The Bottrop district was no exception in this regard. Here, after the appointment of young cadres as the new district leadership in 1950, the former district leaders tried to subvert the authority of the new executive and boycotted its policy.[64] In the end, the conflicts often led to the withdrawal or expulsion of those communist locals who lost the struggle for predominance at the local level.⁶⁵ On a more abstract level, the generational conflicts point to different political experiences and lifestyles which were hard to reconcile within the party culture.

More generally, in the late 1940s the tensions between the older communists and new members which had been simmering since 1945 increasingly developed into open conflicts. Former members of the left-wing splinter parties of the late Weimar Republic became the a special target for criticism. To the communist hardliners, this group represented an unreliable and therefore dangerous element within the party at a time of an alleged heightening of the class struggle. Appeals by the party leadership to overcome the 'mistrust and intolerance which the persons involved have preserved with much skill from before 1933' and not to 'eye each other with suspicion' had only little effect.⁶⁶ On the contrary, with the party headquarters calling for the 'purification' of the organisation and the expulsion of all 'party enemies', many communist locals felt that the time had come to settle old scores and remove their rivals from the party ranks. In the southern German towns of Mannheim and Reutlingen, for example, bitter fights between hostile groups developed in the local organisations which led to numerous expulsions and voluntary resignations from the party ranks.⁶⁷ The purges of the late 1940s and early 1950s were sponsored by the East Berlin headquarters, but they also were appropriated by the rank and file in the West to foster their own interests.

The inner-party struggle had diverse effects on the membership. First of all, a smaller group of communists kept on fighting with energy and conviction for the proclaimed party goals. They supported the tactical moves of the party leadership and constituted the backbone of the KPD in the 1950s up to the banning of the party in 1956 and during the time of illegality. Almost all of these hardcore communists held posts within the party and a high proportion was supported by party funds. After the banning of the party, a number of them moved permanently to the GDR.

The majority of the members who had entered the party only in 1945, as well as a number of party veterans, left the party or were forced out of it at the end of the 1940s. They had found it almost impossible to integrate into the hermetic and well-guarded party culture and were frustrated with the dependance of the KPD on the East German government.

Finally, the majority of those communists who stayed in the party kept their communist faith, but slowly detached themselves from the demands of the party. In the years after 1947, party officials increasingly reported sentiments of 'fatigue' and 'political powerlessness' among the members. Many party veterans felt 'worn out' after long years of fruitless struggle. Often, intense activism suddenly turned into a state of depression and agony.⁶⁸ Also, frequent hints at alcohol abuse by party secretaries indicate that many communists were frustrated with party demands which they often could not reconcile with their traditional political value system. The high-pressure, political persecution to which the communists were subjected reinforced the withdrawal from the party. After 1947, many communists shrank back from political work or even left the party because they feared to be sacked by their employers. State employees especially left the party. In the late 1940s, the party headquarters noticed widespread 'fears of repression, penalising, and arrests' within the party.[69] Finally, the gradual improvement of living conditions had an impact on the party membership. In Dortmund, for example, the party was concerned in 1953 about the effects that compensation payments for political persecution under National Socialism had on the party veterans: 'A lot of them have built up refreshment kiosks and have withdrawn completely from political work'.[70] This retreat into privacy did not automatically mean a giving up of communist convictions, but, in the long run, it furthered a detachment from the Communist Party.

With the division of Germany and the emergence of the SED as the East German supreme ruling state-party, a widening rift can be analysed between the new interests of the SED and traditional communist politics. As my previous examples underline, the KPD cannot be decribed as a monolithic entity. In essence, the postwar KPD was both a tightly organised cadre party and a party rooted in a local urban milieu. To be more specific, while the structure of the West German KPD followed the cadre model on a national level, locally the party organisation often proved beholden to the will of its local members.

These differing political conceptions over the direction and goals of the party placed increasingly conflicting demands on party members. Different interests, world-views and values stood alongside and in opposition to each other. The more the West German KPD succumbed to the wishes of the SED in party organisation and policy, the more West German communist party members silently withdrew their support for the party executive and hindered the execution of party orders. Ultimately, squaring the circle proved impossible for the West German KPD and by the early 1950s the KPD had already eliminated itself as a serious political actor, well before the party's enemies in the Federal Republic had the chance to do so formally in 1956.

Notes

1. See especially Patrick Major, *Death of the KPD. Communism and Anti-Communism in West-Germany*, London 1997. See also as an overview: Dietrich Staritz, 'Die Kommunistische Partei Deutschlands', in Richard Stöss (ed.), *Parteien-Handbuch. Die Parteien der Bundesrepublik Deutschland 1945–1980* (Opladen, 1983), pp.1663–809.

2. See especially Klaus-Michael Mallmann, *Kommunisten in der Weimarer Republik. Sozialgeschichte einer revolutionären Bewegung*, Darmstadt 1996; Eric D. Weitz, *Creating German Communism, 1870–1990. From Popular Protest to Socialist State*, Princeton 1997. For a critical assessment of Mallmann's work see: Andreas Wirsching, 'Stalinisierung' oder entideologisierte 'Nischengesellschaft'? Alte Einsichten und neue Thesen zum Charakter der KPD in der Weimarer Republik', in: *Vierteljahreshefte für Zeitgeschichte* 45 (1997), pp.449–66. For recent discussions of the milieu-concept in historiographical research see: Chrostoph Kösters und Antonius Liedhegener, 'Historische Milieus als Forschungsaufgabe. Zwischenbilanz und Perspektiven', in: *Westfälische Forschungen* 48 (1998), pp.593–601; Franz Walter und Helge Matthiesen, 'Milieus in der modernen deutschen Gesellschaftsgeschichte. Ergebnisse und Perspektiven der Forschung', in: Detlef Schmiechen-Ackermann (ed.), *Anpassung, Verweigerung, Widerstand. Soziale Milieus, Politische Kultur und der Widerstand gegen den Nationalsozialismus in Deutschland im regionalen Vergleich* (Berlin 1997), pp.46–75; Klaus Tenfelds, 'Historische Milieus—Erblichkeit und Konkurrenz', in Manfred Hettling and Paul Nolte (eds), *Nation und Gesellschaft in Deutschland. Historische Essays* (München, 1996), pp.247–68.
3. See: Detlev Peukert, *Die KPD im Widerstand. Verfolgung und Untergrundarbeit an Rhein und Ruhr 1933 bis 1945* (Wuppertal, 1980); Horst Duhnke, *Die KPD von 1933 bis 1945* (Köln, 1972); Klaus-Michael Mallmann, 'Konsistenz oder Zusammenbruch? Profile des kommunistischen Widerstandes 1933–1945', in Detlef Schmiechen-Ackermann (ed.), *Anpassung, Verweigerung, Widerstand. Soziale Milieus, Politische Kultur und der Widerstand gegen den Nationalsozialismus in Deutschland im regionalen Vergleich* (Berlin, 1997), pp.221–37.
4. See: Hermann Weber, *'Weiße Flecken' in der Geschichte. Die KPD-Opfer der Stalinschen Säuberungen und ihre Rehabilitierung.* (Frankfurt/Main, 1989); Hermann Weber und Ulrich Mählert (eds.), *Terror. Stalinistische Parteisäuberungen 1936 bis 1953* (Paderborn, 1998).
5. All membership information is taken from: Till Kössler, 'KPD/DKP/SEW', in: Josef Boyer and Till Kössler (eds), *Parteien in Deutschland, Die Parteien des linken Spektrums. Ein Handbuch zur Mitgliedschaft und Sozialstruktur* (Düsseldorf, 2002). The book is the result of a larger project in which data on party members and functionaries of the political parties in West Germany between 1945 and 1990 was collected and edited.
6. Kössler, 'KPD/DKP/SEW'.
7. For the Weimar party culture and its legacy see Weitz, pp.233–79, 357–8; Detlev Peuckert, *Die KPD im Widerstand. Verfolgung und Untergrundarbeit an Rhein und Ruhr 1933–1945* (Wuppertal, 1980), p.57 ff. For a case study on the emergence of the communist movement: Larry Peterson, *German Communism, Worker's Protest, and Labor Unions. The politics of the United Front in Rhineland-Westphalia, 1920–1924* (London, 1993).
8. Analysis of our work among women in 1949, SAPMO/BA, BY 1/56.
9. See e.g. Police Report Oberhausen, 31 May 1954, Hauptstaatsarchiv Düsseldorf,

Kalkum Branch, Gerichte Rep. 187/56. See also the description of such a dynasty: Ludger Fittkau (ed.), *Das 20. Jahrhundert der Gaudigs. Chronik einer Arbeiterfamilie im Ruhrgebiet* (Essen, 1997).

10. For a political history of the FDJ see: Michael Herms, *Die Westarbeit der FDJ*, (Berlin, 2001); Michael Herms and Gert Noack, 'Die Westarbeit der FDJ 1945/46 bis 1953', in *Deutschlandarchiv*, 28 (1995), pp.1152–61.
11. Peter Henne, Preliminary report on party work in Hattingen district, 17 April 1953, Stiftung Archiv der Parteien und Massenorganisationen der DDR im Bundesarchiv Berlin (SAPMO/BA), BY 1/985. See also on the perserverance of communist mining communities: Wolfgang Jäger, *Bergarbeitermilieus und Parteien im Ruhrgebiet. Zum Wahlverhalten des katholischen Bergarbeitermilieus bis 1933* (München, 1996), especially pp.253 ff.
12. The quotation is taken from a circular of the 'Gemeinschaftshilfe' [Communityhelp] North Rhine-Westfalia, the charity institution of the KPD which in many places took over tasks of the party after its banning in 1956; Circular, 5 February1959, HStA Düsseldorf, Kalkum Branch, Gerichte Rep. 372/786.
13. Kössler, 'KPD/DKP/SEW'.
14. Klaus-Michael Mallmann, 'Die geschlagenen Sieger. Kommunistischer Widerstand an der Saar und im Exil 1933–1945', in Klaus-Michael Mallmann and Gerhard Paul (eds), *Milieus im Widerstand. Eine Verhaltensgeschichte der Gesellschaft im Nationalsozialismus* (Bonn, 1995), p.367. See as a literary account Wolfgang Langhoff, *Die Moorsoldaten* (Zürich, 1936).
15. August Stoetzel, Report on the activity of our party in the Ruhr, May/June 1945, *ibid.*, BY 1/210.
16. Walter Jarreck, Report on the new start of the communists in the Ruhr valley, 1966, *ibid.*, NY 4183/8, p.39.
17. Arnold Sywottek, *Deutsche Volksdemokratie. Studien zur politischen Konzeption der KPD 1935–1946* (Düsseldorf, 1971); Peter Erler, Horst Laude, *et al.*(eds), '*Nach Hitler kommen wir*'. *Dokumente und Programmatik der Moskauer KPD-Führung 1944/45 für Nachkriegsdeutschland* (Berlin, 1994).
18. See especially Staritz, 'Die Kommunistische Partei Deutschlands', pp.1677–87.
19. Walter Jarreck, Report on the new start of the communists in the Ruhr valley, 1966, SAPMO/BA, NY 4183/8, p.53. For resistance in the rank and file see Report on the district Niederrhein, 13 August1945, ibid., NY 4036/635.
20. Report of the political secretary of the Ruhr valley district on the period 15 April-1 August 1945, ibid., BY 1/210.
21. Strang to Bevin, 20 December 1945, Public Record Office (Kew), FO 1049/322.
22. Party statues 1951 (Document 16), in: Guenter Judick, Josef Schleifstein and Kurt Steinhaus (eds), *KPD 1945–1968. Dokumente*, 2 vols (Neuss, 1989).
23. Report by the party executive, Ruhr-Westfalen district, 23 February 1946, SAPMO/BA, BY 1/576.
24. See Karin Hartewig, 'Wolf unter Wölfen? Die prekäre Macht der kommunistischen Kapos im Konzentrationslager Buchenwald', in Ulrich Herbert *et al.*

(eds), *Die nationalsozialistischen Konzentrationslager. Entwicklung und Struktur* (Göttingen, 1998), pp.939–58.
25. Report of the Ruhr district executive, 25 August1945, SAPMO/BA, BY 1/210.
26. Walter Jarreck and Hans Schiwon, Report on the party in the Ruhr-district, April to July 1945, *ibid.*, BY 1/212.
27. Report by the district executive Speyer at the instructor and district conference Rhineland-Palatinate, 26 January 1949, ibid., BY 1/1054.
28. Report on the Ruhr-district, 20 September 1945, ibid., BY 1/210.
29. 1 Corps, Political Intelligence Report, 24 November 1945, PRO FO 1049/2112.
30. Political Intelligence Report, 11 August1945, PRO FO 371/46934.
31. Intelligence Division Summary, 30 October 1946, PRO FO 1005/1702.
32. Report by the party executive, Ruhr-Westfalen district, 15 April-1 August 1945, SAPMO/BA, BY 1/210.
33. Minutes of the zone executive meeting, 29 January 1947, SAPMO/BA, BY 1/709.
34. For the official party line see Aufruf des Zentralkomitees vom 11. Juni 1945, in Ossip K. Flechtheim, *Dokumente zur parteipolitischen Entwicklung in Deutschland seit 1945*, 3. Band, pp.313–18.
35. Intelligence Report No. 1, 12 December 1945, PRO FO 1005/1700.
36. Report on the district Niederrhein, 13 August 1945, SAPMO/BA, NY 4036/635.
37. British Consulate Bremen, Political and Economic Report on Land Bremen, December 1947, PRO FO 371/70482.
38. Intelligence Division Summary No. 10, 30 November 1946, PRO FO 1005/1702.
39. Michael Lemke, *Einheit oder Sozialismus. Die Deutschlandpolitik der SED 1949–1961* (Köln, 2001), especially p.12; Heike Amos, *Die Westpolitik der SED 1948/49–1961. 'Arbeit nach Westdeutschland' durch die Nationale Front, das Ministerium für Auswärtige Angelegenheiten und das Ministerium für Staatssicherheit.* (Berlin, 1999).
40. See for the following Michael Kubina, 'Was in dem einen Teil verwirklicht werden kann mit Hilfe der Roten Armee, wird im anderen Teil Kampffrage sein.' Zum Aufbau des zentralen Westapparates der KPD/SED 1945–1949', in: Manfred Wilke (ed.), *Die Anatomie der Parteizentrale. Die KPD/SED auf dem Weg zur Macht* (Berlin 1998), pp.413–500; Lemke, *Einheit oder Sozialismus*, especially pp.58–68.
41. See notes of Wilhelm Pieck, 23.10.1946, SAPMO/BA NY 4036/643. See also for the following Major, *Death of the KPD*, pp.64f.
42. Walter Fisch, memorandum, 2.10.1946, SAPMO/BA, NY 4182/862.
43. See especially Herbert Mayer, 'Nur eine Wahlniederlage? Zum Verhältnis SED und KPD in den Jahren 1948/49', in: Wilfriede Otto (ed.), '*Die Waldheimer Prozesse*' 1950 (Berlin, 1993), pp.29–46.
44. Cited Major, *Death of the KPD*, p.68.
45. Amos, pp.340–2; Lemke, *Einheit oder Sozialismus*, pp.55–7; Kubina, 'Was in dem einen Teil verwirklicht werden kann mit Hilfe der Roten Armee, wird im

anderen Teil Kampffrage sein'. See also Josef Kaiser, 'Der politische Gewinn steht in keinem Verhältnis zum Aufwand. Zur Westarbeit des FDGB im Kalten Krieg', in *Jahrbuch für Kommunismusforschung* 1996, pp.106–31.
46. Kössler, 'KPD/DKP/SEW'.
47. SED West-commission, evaluation of the Federal Elections in West-Germany, September 1949, SAPMO, BA BY 1/468.
48. Lemke, *Einheit oder Sozialismus*, p.17. For the broader picture see Dietrich Staritz, *Geschichte der DDR* (Frankfurt/Main, 1995), S. 84–94.
49. Report on the situation in the West and the role of the KPD, 6 April 1948, SAPMO/BA, BY 1/563.
50. Report of the Ruhr district executive, 25 August 1945, SAPMO/BA, BY 1/210.
51. See e.g. letter of the party executive Lower Saxony to all Zehnergruppenleiter, Hannover, 11 January 1949, SAPMO/BA, BY 1/195.
52. Report on the party organisation, 1953, SAPMO/BA, BY 1/567.
53. A. Zeidler, report on the party development, 8 February 1951, SAPMO/BA, BY 1/566. For a local case study see: Hendrik Bunke, 'Die Reinigung der Partei...' Auseinandersetzungen in der Bremer KPD 1951/52', in *Arbeiterbewegung und Sozialgeschichte. Zeitschrift für die Regionalgeschichte Bremens im 19. und 20. Jahrhundert* 2 (1998), pp.5–24.
54. Major, *Death of the KPD*, pp.201–10; Herbert Mayer, *Durchsetzt von Parteifeinden, Agenten, Verbrechern...? Zu den Parteisäuberungen in der KPD (1948–1952) und der Mitwirkung der SED* (Berlin, 1995); Ulrich Heyden, 'Säuberungen in der KPD 1948 bis 1951', in Wolfgang Maderthaner, Hans Schafranek and Berthold Unfried (eds), *'Ich habe den Tode verdient'. Schauprozesse und politische Verfolgung in Mittel- und Osteuropa 1945–1956* (Wien, 1991), pp.139–58.
55. Report on a meeting of the comrades Ledwohn, Jennes and Bönsch of North Rhine-Westfalia, 20 March 1950, SAPMO/BA, BY 1/565.
56. Political report on organisation matters, 17 May 1951, SAPMO/BA, BY 1/1027.
57. Report on Wuerttemberg-Hohenzollern, 1951, SAPMO/BA, BY 1/1027.
58. For a detailed portrayal of the national policy see Michael Klein, *Antifaschistische Demokratie und nationaler Befreiungskampf. Die nationale Politik der KPD 1949–1953* (Berlin, 1986).
59. Max Reimann, Report on the General Elections in the West, 20 August 1949, SAPMO/BA, NY 4036/643.
60. Report on the ideological situation of the KPD, 18 November 1952, SAPMO/BA, BY 1/570.
61. Report by the working committee of the KPD, 23 January 1954, SAPMO/BA.
62. Report on the improvement of the internal party affairs, 1952, SAPMO/BA, BY 1/567.
63. Report on the party youth, 1949, SAPMO/BA, BY 1/57.
64. See the instructors report of Fritz Taraschewski, 9 March 1950, SAPMO/BA, BY 1/988.
65. SAPMO/BA, BY 1/988, 17 March 1950 and 30 March 1950.

66. District executive Bocholt to district office Westfalen-North, 13 March 1948, SAPMO/BA, DY 30/IV 2/10.02/247.
67. Political Report Reutlingen, 10 July 1951, SAPMO/BA, BY 1/1027.
68. See statement Hugo Paul, 4. meeting of the party executive, August 1948, SAPMO/BA, BY 1/425; Political analysis of the membership of the KPD in the West, 1950, SAPMO/BA, BY 1/573. See also Mallmann, *Geschlagene Sieger*, p.524. I have examined the process of 'de-radicalisation' of the communists in West Germany in the essay: Till Kössler, 'Zwischen militanter Tradition und Zivilgesellschaft. Die Kommunisten in Westdeutschland 1945–1960', in Thomas Kühne (ed.), *Von der Kriegskultur zur Friedenskultur? Zum Mentalitätswandel in Deutschland seit 1945* (Münster, 2000), pp.219–42.
69. SED-west section, situation report on the KPD, 8 November 1948, SAPMO/BA, BY 1/65. For an overview of the persecution of the communists in the Federal Republic see Alexander von Brünneck, *Politische Justiz gegen Kommunisten in der Bundesrepublik Deutschland 1949–1968* (Frankfurt/Main, 1978).
70. Report of comrade Walter Krzyzanowski on his operation in western Germany, 14 August 1953, SAPMO/BA, BY 1/570.

Cypriot, Indian and West Indian Branches of the CPGB, 1945–1970

An experiment in self-organisation?

Andrew Flinn

> The approach of Marxists to questions of culture and nationality was one which did not want people to forget their origins and language. But at the same time it was necessary to face up to questions of common struggle in this country...
>
> *Betty Matthews, London organiser*[1]

Since its inception the membership of the Communist Party of Great Britain (CPGB) always reflected some of the ethnic and national diversity of the British working class. As well as the English core, some of the party's earliest and most consistent supporters came from the mining and industrial centres of South Wales and Scotland. Irish immigrants, often with a nationalist background, also joined the party. Like many other communist parties, a substantial part of the CPGB's membership was also drawn from Jewish immigrants and their descendants who had left eastern Europe at the end of the nineteenth and beginning of the twentieth centuries. In some areas, where Jewish communities were concentrated, such as Stepney in the East End of London and Cheetham Hill in Manchester, Jewish members were in the majority in local parties. Small numbers of workers and students from Empire countries and elsewhere were also to be found in the pre-war party.

After the Second World War, large numbers of immigrants from Europe and the colonies and former colonies, notably the West Indies and the Indian sub-continent, came to Britain. A number of these, often with experience in the Labour movements of their native countries, joined the CPGB. In the context of a diverse ethnic membership, the party had to face questions of race and class, strategies to oppose racism, and demands for self-organisation and self-determination. This article, rather than attempting to examine the entire history of the relationship of the CPGB and ethnic/national identities, will concentrate on one particular episode—the emergence and subsequent dissolution of branches based, not on residence or the workplace, but on national identity.

Apart from Hakim Adi's account of the Nigerian and West African branches very little has been written about the national branches.[2] The party acquiesced in their existence rather than openly acknowledging them. In 1965 a national committee on party organisation, despite focusing on branch structures and dealing with women's and youth representation, made no reference to the existence of these branches, not even to recommend their dissolution. The following year—in which the Indian and Cypriot branches were closed down—Jack Woddis, head of the CPGB's international department, claimed that the party had decided to dissolve the Indian branches as it had only just discovered their existence. In fact, since 1945 the party had been aware of and had turned a blind eye to the evolution of a whole network of organisations based on nationality. These varied from a formal branch and organisational structure like that possessed by the Indian and London Cypriot branches to the smaller, often ad hoc groups or branches that included comrades from the West Indies, West Africa, Ceylon, South Africa and Mauritius.[3]

Records of these branches are hard to find and their life was often short. When, on occasions, the party attempted to block their formation—for example, permission for a West African branch in Liverpool was refused—the existence of such branches was well known and justified by reference to 'exceptional' circumstances:

> Thus the West African branch, was only formed temporarily in a special situation, which is now drawing to a close; and the necessity of special Cypriot branches arose on the question of language.

In this article I will examine the development and fate of Cypriot, Indian and West Indian branches. I will also offer some suggestions as to what this tells us about the expression of national identity within the CPGB, the case for separate representation and self-determination for different identities, the influence of international developments on non-British party members and the CPGB's concern to preserve unity and exclude dissent.[4]

The Cypriot branches

Before the war London had a small Cypriot population. However, against the background of the political and economic problems which beset British-controlled Cyprus in the immediate postwar period, Cypriot immigration grew rapidly. In 1950 there were about 7000 Cypriots living in London. By 1966, estimates put the Cypriot population in Greater London as between

50,000 and 70,000 with perhaps a further 30,000 living elsewhere in Britain. The large majority of this community was Greek but there was also a significant Turkish population. As a new immigrant group within an 'alien' country (and particularly without a common language), the Cypriots remained a relatively insular community. Close links were retained with families on Cyprus. Many regularly sent money home and indeed intended to return to Cyprus in the very near future. The vast majority of the immigrants were working class, concentrated in small (often Cypriot-owned) clothing and catering businesses.[5]

Speaking little English and having minimal contact with the indigenous culture, Cypriots were not very active in labour movement institutions such as the trade unions or the co-operatives. However, the struggles for independence in Cyprus and against fascism in Greece meant that they came from a highly politicised culture. Many had been active supporters or members of the Progressive Party of Working People (AKEL), which had succeeded the Cypriot Communist Party in 1941. Cypriots in England continued to campaign against British rule and after a limited form of independence was granted by the 1960 Zurich-London Agreement, the struggle focused on the continued domination of the island by British and American interests, notably the imposition of NATO bases.

Given their level of politicisation and support for AKEL, many Cypriot immigrants continued their involvement in communist politics in Britain. Originally members of the small Cypriot community joined the London section of AKEL. In 1947 the decision was taken to close down the London section and its members were advised to join the CPGB. According to Evdoros Joannides, the CPGB's international department agreed that Cypriot comrades should concentrate on their economic and political struggles amongst the Cypriot community.[6]

The separation of Cypriot members from normal party life and campaigns was formalised by the unusual, but by no means unique, decision to allow the creation of national branches. The formation of Cypriot branches was justified in two ways. First, in order to combat the language problem— very few Cypriots had more than rudimentary English at this time—the branches were to use Greek or Turkish. Secondly, as the liberation of Cyprus was considered to be imminent, it was believed that most members would soon return to Cyprus. Initial membership was around fifty. In the early years there were residential branches as well as industrial branches in catering and tailoring. Ten years later there were 450 members in London. By 1966 London District had 30 Cypriot branches with 1,200 members, with another 300 members in YCL branches. This represented something approaching a fifth of the total district membership. According to Max Egelnick, a leading London party member, the Cypriots were 'our biggest single group of comrades in London.' Although the branches were overwhelmingly concentrated in the capital, there were also branches in Liverpool and Cardiff.[7]

As well as the branches, over a number of years a formal party structure developed which was increasingly independent of the district or even the national party. Branch activities were co-ordinated by an elected leadership, the Cypriot guiding committee (GC). The GC was elected by the Cypriot membership at biennial delegate conferences and also provided the movement with officers and a secretariat. The committee also administered its own publishing house and supervised the production of a Greek language newspaper, *VEMA*. To all intents and purposes, the Cypriot branches operated as a separate district or even as a party within the CPGB. At successive Cypriot conferences in 1963 and 1965, the branches voted to strengthen their structures and as a consequence their independence from the parent party. A report by a London district official noted that moves at the 1965 conference revealed 'a desire to limit the influence of the British party.'[8]

As a result of these developments and the political committee's determination to dissolve the Indian branches, in 1966 London district was instructed to close down the Cypriot branches and transfer the membership to existing residential and workplace branches. The party leadership presented the principles at stake as clear and non-negotiable. They gave as examples the experiences in pre-revolutionary Russia, in Austria and the USA that indicated that organisation on the basis of nationality led to isolation and disunity within the working class-movement. Whilst recognising the difficulties of 'the bringing together of different nationalities', the party insisted on the strict application of the rules which allowed for 'only one basic unit in an enterprise or a locality, and only one party leadership at higher levels'. Despite the warnings of the district secretary John Mahon that without careful handling it could result in the loss of hundreds of members, unification of the branches was implemented.[9]

The decision to dissolve the branches was initially supported by many Cypriot activists. Many of them, particularly those leaders who were also active in the CPGB, were initially strong advocates of unification. George Pefkos, at that time editor of *VEMA*, continued to advocate unification for years as a way of counteracting Cypriot isolation from the rest of the working class. Another leading Cypriot comrade acknowledged that there should not be two parties in Britain, saying that 'We Cypriots are here and we must be in one Party with the other British comrades'.

It was generally agreed that the separation of branches was aggravating a tendency for Cypriot communists 'to work only among Cypriots' and not to participate in the activities of the CPGB and the wider labour movement. Equally, British comrades did not involve themselves in campaigns within the Cypriot community because that was seen as the responsibility of Cypriot members. The party acknowledged the problems of language and culture but invoked the examples of Marx, Engels and Lenin who through their willingness to learn English had played an active role in the British labour movement. The GC supported these arguments with only one dissenting vote. When unification was recommended to the branches, 265 members voted in favour with only 33 against.[10]

In spite of the positive welcome given to unification by many Cypriot leaders, the actual outcome was judged by many to have been a disaster. Within four years the party had lost 500 Cypriot members. By 1980 a list of Cypriot members in London numbered less than 200, a decline which far outstripped the fall in the party's total membership.[11] Immediately after unification was announced, the party was warned that because of the language and cultural differences involved, the process must be treated as a political task, not just as an administrative re-organisation. However, this was exactly what happened. Unification was implemented but very little was done to ensure its success.[12]

The outstanding problems could not be avoided a year later in 1967. Branch after branch reported a lack of participation by Cypriot members. Stoke Newington branch, where previously there had been over 80 Cypriot members, said it was impossible to persuade them to attend the unified branch meetings because:

> they say they won't come if there is a Cypriot speaker because they know it already and won't come if there is an English speaker because they can't understand.

A leading Cypriot later commented that those Stoke Newington meetings were conducted entirely in English and those Cypriots who had turned up initially left without having said a word or understood the proceedings. The language question was an over-riding problem. Few branches were able to provide interpreters and those that did, like the Rectory branch in Hackney, found the process 'to be very tedious' and divisive. Certainly there seem to be indications that the branches were less welcoming to their new members than they might have been.[13]

Another problem highlighted the difference in attitudes between the Cypriot leadership and the mass membership. Leaders like Pefkos and Hambis Mitchell, who had promoted unification of the branches, were much more integrated into the structures and work of the CPGB than was the average Cypriot member. Both Pefkos and Mitchell held positions on the district committee and were (or had been) members of the national party's international committee. The primary interest of most Cypriot members however remained not in the policies of the CPGB or issues of domestic British politics but in events in Cyprus and Greece. Additionally domestic, working and cultural practices within the Cypriot community meant that regular attendance at branch meetings was neither easy nor considered to be a core responsibility of party membership. Some years later Egelnick commented that for many Cypriots, the label 'communist' had much a much broader and less formal, organisational meaning than for British communists. The content of the branch meetings was also the cause for discontent. Andreas Kleanthous, active in Stoke Newington, unfavourably contrasted the dry business agendas of most British meetings with the mix of the theoretical and the practical that Cypriots were accustomed to.[14]

It was also pointed out that in unification the party was attempting to overcome a much wider social isolation in which the Cypriots had little contact with English society and vice versa. Even the institutions of the labour movement, such as the trade unions and the co-operatives, were not seen as offering anything to the Cypriot community. This wider division was reflected in the CPGB in that few Cypriots believed that the British party understood their problems or could represent their interests.[15]

By 1968, although leading comrades such as Pefkos, Yiasemides and Zavros continued to argue the case for unification, others such as Mitchell, Tsioupras and the Turkish Cypriot leader Sadi were advocating the re-establishment of some form of separate organisation. Given the reality of the growing numbers of Cypriots withdrawing from active political involvement, the district leadership also began to review the situation. Initially proposals were made for branches to hold occasional additional meetings in Greek. Belated efforts were made by the British party to campaign within the Cypriot community, for instance by translating party statements into Greek and developing a specific programme reflecting the interests and problems of the community. Subsequent plans included Cypriot groups (within branches) meeting regularly and electing officers who would represent them on branch committees. By the summer of 1970 a London district document on 'Problems of Cypriot membership' openly acknowledged that the leadership of many English branches agreed with their Cypriot comrades that the problems could only 'be resolved by a separation of the Cypriot membership in every respect.' The district recommended reformation of separate branches with an elected leadership responsible to their borough committees. However when these proposals were put to three leading Cypriot comrades, Pefkos, Mitchell and Tsioupras, all three rejected them. Mitchell and Tsioupras wanted complete separation and Pefkos continued to advocate unification. In any case when the proposals were referred to the political committee that body reaffirmed the party's determination to sanction only one unified party structure. Given the widespread antipathy of Cypriot members to participation within the unified structures of the CPGB, it is hardly surprising that in 1972 AKEL informed the party's London district committee that it planned to re-open its London branch.[16]

At a superficial level it seems that the dissolution of the Cypriot branches and the end of separate representation was directly responsible for the decline in Cypriot membership. Unification was rushed through and implemented without much conviction by either English or Cypriot comrades. Hambis Mitchell argued that at the time of unification 'co-operation between the Cypriots and the English branches was practically non-existent...[and] neither the Cypriots nor the British comrades were ready for it.' To Kleanthous language remained a major stumbling block to unity. He maintained that no real provision had been made for translation to help overcome the problem. In another ten or fifteen years the next generation, more confident in English, might be able to participate fully in a unified party. In the meantime, the critics of unification argued, the party's principles relating to unitary organisation were responsible not for strengthening the membership but for driving away Cypriot members.[17]

However, a closer reading of the evidence suggests that language, and thus unification, was not the only or even the main problem. After unification, a few branches (in Haringey and Islington) had memberships that were predominantly Cypriot, had elected Cypriot officers and conducted their meetings in Greek. However these branches also showed low levels of participation and activity. It was argued by some that unification provided a convenient opportunity to resign or lapse from membership for those Cypriots whose participation in and loyalty to the CPGB was already minimal or declining. Evidence suggested that mass Cypriot participation in political issues was already declining before unification and had been since independence in 1960. Although a large majority had voted for unification, it is indicative that the total number of Cypriot members who actually participated in this vote was low.[18]

Those who did remain active in mass campaigns tended to remain focused on international issues rather than British politics. At the same time as unification, a broad-based mass movement called the Union of Cypriots in Britain (UCB) was established to co-ordinate solidarity campaigns within the Cypriot community. Staffed almost entirely by Cypriot members, the party subsequently became concerned that comrades were concentrating all their energies in the UCB and neglecting other party work. Developments in internal Cypriot and Greek politics had always been influential and sometimes divisive within the Cypriot branches. Disputes within AKEL over the nature of the liberation struggle and alliances with non-working class forces led to periodic splits and resignations within the British party. On occasions the stance taken by AKEL on an international issue differed from that taken by the CPGB, again causing problems. According to London organiser Ernie Clarke, the CPGB's and AKEL's contrary lines on the Soviet action in Czechoslovakia in 1968 resulted in 'considerable problems in retaining the membership' of some Cypriot members.[19]

The next section will show that the Indian branches were closed down because they had begun to act as a separate structure within the party and were advocating a line that in the context of the divisions in the international communist movement was in opposition to that of the CPGB. At least one Cypriot activist also thought that the real target of unification was not the principle of unified organisation as much as the power and political independence of the Cypriot GC.[20]

The Indian branches

As with the Cypriot community, small numbers of Indian workers and students had long had a presence in England and had been active in Indian and communist organisations. However, it was the post-war period and particularly the 1950s which saw mass immigration to Britain from India. The need of these new immigrants for practical aid and support in an alien and increasingly hostile environment saw the re-establishment and flourishing of the Indian Workers' Association (IWA). Some of the new arrivals such as Abhimanyu Manchanda and Vishnu Sharma had been active in the Communist Party of India (CPI) and they and others joined the CPGB. In some areas such as Leamington Spa, Indian members were responsible for reviving an essentially moribund local movement.[21]

In May 1956 the CPGB's international department responded to the new developments by establishing a co-ordinating committee of leading Indian party members. This committee, operating under the auspices of the international department, was to advise the party on its work in the Indian community in Britain, particularly with respect to building up the IWAs. According to the party, this committee was always intended to be of a 'temporary and limited character.' At the same time the international department issued a document advising Indian party members, while remaining active branch members, to form local Indian groups. These groups would aid members:

> to arrive at an unified understanding of the problems of Indian workers and to carry out Party policy in the IWA...Closer contact with the movement in India and the Party and study of problems relating to them will also be possible.

These groups were to be responsible to district authority. In effect this was an organisational recognition by the party of the special interests of Indian members.[22]

Over the next ten years, the co-ordinating committee and the Indian groups developed into a much more formal, permanent structure. Membership was concentrated in London, West Middlesex and Midlands districts but Indian members were also to be found in the East Midlands, Yorkshire and Lancashire. The committee appointed officers, established a secretariat, attempted to call conferences and directed the activities of the party's Indian membership. In the eyes of the party the co-ordinating committee had begun to act as an 'alternative political leadership'. The groups began to act as branches, parallel to the existing residential branches, with a wholly Indian membership. According to Ramdin, these branches mostly focused on issues relating to Indian politics and rarely discussed matters relating to the CPGB's policies or programmes. There was some confusion over the status of these branches. In 1966 the party leadership claimed that they had never approved the establishment of Indian branches. However, previously a loyal party member such as Vishnu Sharma had openly advertised his membership and leadership of the Southall Indian branch in his 1961 executive committee nomination. Party leader John Gollan stated that some Indian branches such as Southall had been sanctioned, like the Cypriot branches, 'where there is a language difficulty and where there are clearly defined concentrations of such workers'. According to Woddis, all these developments were equivalent to 'setting up a separate Indian organisation, with its own rules and regulations, within the general body of our Party.'[23]

What particularly concerned the party was the extent to which the Indian branches had become embroiled in disputes within the IWA and the wider Indian community. These arguments were mostly centred on the IWA in Southall and involved party members on both sides. Whilst these disputes initially concerned the control of organisations and assets in Southall, they also developed, in the context of the splits within the CPI and in the international communist movement, a political dimension. In Southall the party branch and the IWA was led by CPGB member and supporter of the original CPI,

Vishnu Sharma. This group was opposed by leading members of the co-ordinating committee and national officers of the IWA such as Manchanda, Jagmohan Joshi, Sohan Singh Sandhu, Ranjana Ash, and Rattan Singh. These comrades generally took a pro-Chinese line in the international communist movement disputes and supported the breakaway CPI (Marxist) party in India. From 1963, this grouping took an increasingly hostile stance towards the CPGB. They accused the party of betraying 'proletarian internationalism' and supporting the 'revisionist Dangeite clique' of the CPI. They claimed that the CPGB had been encouraging the 'stooge Vishnu group' in the disruption of the IWA. Sandhu, Joshi and Manchanda all attended the pro-Chinese 11th World Conference Against Atom and Hydrogen Bombs in Tokyo in 1965.[24]

The leading elements in the co-ordinating committee were also hostile to the CPGB's activity in Britain on Indian issues and racial discrimination. Disappointed with the party's failure to organise support for an IWA rally against the treatment of political prisoners in India, Joshi and Sandhu made contact with the Trotskyist Young Socialists, culminating with Dutt being heckled by this group at an IWA rally. They also took a more militant attitude to the 'racialism' of the Labour government's immigration policy. Whereas Sharma agreed to sit on the national committee for Commonwealth immigrants, the co-ordinating committee advocated a boycott of all such organisations. In the 1966 General Election, Joshi and Sandhu called on Indian and other immigrant voters to abstain in constituencies where there was not an avowedly anti-racist candidate. Both stances ran contrary to CPGB policy.[25]

In 1963 Manchanda and a number of others argued that because of the special features of the struggles of the victims of national and racial oppression and the 'extra intensity' of the exploitation of national minorities, there needed to be a recognition of the necessity for special organisational forms to represent these minorities. To this end he wished to publish a journal, Indian Forum, and to organise Indian communists in a branch around this publication. The party leadership refused permission for this, arguing that:

> your proposal to bring together, from all over London, Indian party members from different factories and localities, and to put them into a separate Indian branch purely on a basis of their nationality...would be the worst kind of Bundism.

Justifiably, the CPGB viewed Manchanda's intention as being to set up a group within the party that was hostile to the CPI and CPGB.[26]

The decision in 1966 to close down the Indian branches and the co-ordinating committee was based on the same analysis. At the meeting of Indian comrades at which the reorganisation was announced on 13 February 1966, Jack Woddis stated that the party was reviewing its organisation in reference to its rules. However the move was not motivated by administrative and organisational concerns but by political ones, notably the desire to close down a forum for damaging internal dissent. The party argued that while it realised that Indian comrades (and indeed all comrades) were entitled to discuss and take a stance on issues affecting the CPI and international communist movement generally, these views should not be expressed publicly through party organisations or machinery. Instead of continued separate organisation, the party reverted to central control and paternalism. Woddis spelt out the party's belief that the appropriate forum for discussions on fighting racism or the development of international solidarity should be in district-appointed advisory committees. Districts would be able to 'add some of our leading Indians members on to these committees to assist in advice on appropriate matters.'[27]

It is not clear whether this re-establishment of centralised control had the same effect on the membership of the Indian branches as on the Cypriot branches. District leaders were instructed to try to keep as many members as possible. There is some evidence of resentment about the branch closures but the main opposition to the move was political. On 11 and 12 June 1966, a meeting was held by the co-ordinating committee of Indian communists in Britain. They denounced the decision and vowed to continue the dissolved branches and committee. Of the 26 present, 25 were still party members while Manchanda had only recently been expelled. Many of these finally resigned in the autumn, following visits from leaders of the CPI (M). Under their influence up to 30 Indian members had resigned from the CPGB by October 1966 to join the newly formed Association of Indian Communists in Great Britain. These splits were worsened by further developments in the Indian communist politics in 1968, and the various groupings remained separate in the late 1980s.[28]

The West Indian branches

While the development of the Cypriot and Indian branches had a clear provenance, the origin and evolution of the West Indian branches was much less clear. The sources that mention the branches refer variously to West Indian groups, branches and committees. The exact relationship between the different organisations is not easily discerned. Certainly in the early 1950s there were a small number of West Indian residential branches in London. One of these, the West London West Indian branch, was based in Earls Court, another was possibly located in South London. These organisations may have been referred to as West Indian committees but there was also a formal committee of the same name that operated under the auspices of the International Department. The West Indian Committee (WIC) was formed in 1949 to help formulate party policy on the West Indies. In addition, aggregate meetings brought together all West Indian members of the CPGB on a regular basis. Estimates of the numbers attending these meetings in the 1950s vary between 50 and 150. Membership included both working-class West Indians, some of whom had experience in trade union and political movements in the Caribbean, and students who were organised in the West Indian Students Union. Like their Cypriot and Indian comrades, an important concern of many of these members, at least initially, was in developments in the countries they had just left.[29]

The fate of the West Indian branches is also somewhat obscure. In the second half of 1955, London district membership records show that all the members of the West Indian branch had been transferred into their 'respective branches in West London'. The following year, the party held an inquiry into the splits and divisions amongst the members of the WIC. The inquiry found against the working practices of one of the committee's leading members, Billy Strachan, and his supporters. Although Strachan remained in the party, he resigned as WIC secretary and from other leading positions within the West Indian mass movement. Over the next few years, West Indian organisations within and around the party lost their cohesion and momentum and black members drifted away from the party. The WIC continued in some form at least until the early 1960s but the branches had disappeared and aggregate meetings were longer called. Some sources maintain that the WIC was disbanded and reformed as an international department advisory committee. Subsequently the party constituted a Caribbean Committee and then a Race Relations Committee to formulate party policy on issues relating to black workers and racism, but these were not the black-only structures that some participants sought.[30]

In the context of the international struggles of the period and the racism in Britain in the 1950s, for many West Indian political activists, 'it seemed natural for the Communist Party to be the home of black militants'. However their experiences within the CPGB forced some of these members to argue for a degree of self-representation. Trevor Carter explains that West Indian branches were formed 'in response to the difficulties faced by many black members in working within the ordinary party framework.' These difficulties had two manifestations. First, that issues important to black members were seemingly ignored by white members, and secondly, that the racist and imperialist attitudes common to white people in general were to be found in the CPGB. In 1957 an international advisory committee memorandum 'West Indians in Britain' castigated the failure of areas and branches to take the problems faced by black workers in Britain seriously. The party published policy documents opposing racial discrimination but did not actively campaign on the issue until later.[31]

Dorothy Kuya, a Liverpool-born woman of African and British parents, was active in the party in both Liverpool and London in the 1950s and 1960s. During this time she came to the conclusion that the party, unlike the African Marxists and the CPUSA whose writings she had begun to read, did not view the issues of race and racism as important within its class perspective. She, along with other comrades, was critical of the CPGB's failure to follow the lead of the American party in developing and promoting black cadres. For many, the party's disregard of race issues was exemplified by its failure to recognise and utilise the skills and experiences of the prominent black communist leader, Claudia Jones, after she was deported to Britain from America in 1955.[32]

While the party's opposition to racism in Britain in the 1950s was seen as theoretical rather than practical, its policies on the Empire and colonial independence movements as outlined in the *British Road to Socialism* were regarded by many black members as chauvinist and imperialist. The first version of the *British Road* clumsily stated that claims that the party's policies meant the destruction of the British Empire were a lie. A later commentary on it by the WIC retorted that:

> We are against Empire, and are for the destruction of the Empire. This is not a lie. The best that can be said about this paragraph is that it is badly worded.

Indeed the next version of the *British Road* dropped the formulation. A more long-running dispute concerned future relations between a socialist Britain and its former colonies. The 1951 *British Road* visualised a 'close fraternal association', slightly amended to a voluntary association and the maintenance of special trading relations. Members of the WIC and others expressed doubts over the 'phraseology' but were reassured by party leaders like Palme Dutt. However, developments in the independence movements meant that at the time of the next *British Road* revision in 1956 the justifications were no longer seen as sustainable. The WIC dismissed 'fraternal association' as an attempt to impose a new form of British-led alliance on newly independent colonies. The committee supported a much looser voluntarist formulation of 'fraternal relations'. The executive committee, however, insisted on maintaining the original formulation until, led by Dutt, the 1957

National Congress defeated them. The impression given to many members from the West Indies and from other (former) colonies was that the party leadership was more interested in the construction of anti-American alliances than respecting the rights of self-determination for colonial peoples. Kuya recalls that the debate over the *British Road to Socialism* first encouraged her doubts in the leadership of the CPGB and stimulated her interest in African Marxists and black politics.[33]

Some argued that the lack of interest and racism of the CPGB demonstrated the need for the formation or continuation of separate organisations. However others such as Chris Le Maitre, like the Cypriot advocates of unification, opposed separate organisation on the grounds that it segregated black members from the rest of the party and legitimised the disregard of issues such as the racial discrimination faced by black workers in Britain by the main body of the movement. Within the WIC itself, there were divisions between students and more working-class members. Strachan and his supporters were hostile to the students and favoured a rigid line of class unity above considerations of race. Others argued for greater independence within the party for black members and their organisations. Trevor Carter believes that one reason the party enquiry found against Strachan was that they believed he would remain loyal to the party if disciplined while the others would leave.[34]

As a result of these divisions and the attitude of the party leadership, a large number of West Indian members became disenchanted with the party. For instance Frank Bailey, a Guyanan who had joined the CPGB in 1954, attacked the failure of the white labour movement to assist colonial liberation struggles and gave his support to an anti-party fraction in the West Indian Association in 1958. Eventually he left the party and became involved in a Trotskyist group within the Labour Party. Others used the party as a forum to promote ideas of pan-Africanism and black power rather than Marxism. As with some Cypriots and Indians, many West Indian members saw their loyalty in terms of the international communist movement rather than the CPGB in particular. So developments internationally, notably the revelations about Stalin, the Caribbean revolution in Cuba and the Sino-Soviet split all resulted in the party losing members.[35]

Chinese support for colonial liberation struggles and opposition to peaceful co-existence attracted many whose interests were international rather than British. For instance John James, another Guyanan who in 1959 was secretary of the WIC and a member of the party's London district colonial committee, was viewed by Claudia Jones and Billy Strachan as a loyal and reliable comrade. In 1963 he was expelled for actively promoting a pro-Chinese and anti-CPGB line around liberation struggles in Asia, the

Caribbean and Africa. In his defence he referred to the party's persecution of 'the most active and militant comrades from the Caribbean'. His branch, the Stoke Newington branch, over half of whom were black, supported his position. A statement issued by members of the branch in support of James and the Chinese position in the international communist movement dispute, claimed that 'we, West Indians are treated like children by the British party'. The party responded to the statement by treating it as an act of resignation. Twelve out of the thirteen signatures on the statement belonged to black comrades.[36]

Not all black members drifted away or actively resigned from the party. A small number remained in the CPGB into the 1980s and later. Loyal to Marxist ideas, they were willing to fight within the party to try to influence its direction. In 1986, the party's leading black member, Trevor Carter, who had joined in 1954 and had been a prominent member of the WIC, believed that the CPGB was beginning to understand the connections 'between socialism and black liberation'. However he concluded that it was a tragedy that this was the same party which had 'lost the allegiance of so many committed black socialists by not listening to them when it had the chance.'[37]

Language, culture and dissent

The twenty-year history of the national branches points to some conclusions about the relationship between the CPGB and different ethnic and national identities as well as the party's inability to accept collective difference or dissent. In the years that followed the end of the Second World War, the party sanctioned, in particular in London, a network of branches based on nationality. Although the existence of these institutions was rarely referred to, it was well known. The branches were justified on the grounds that either language or some other temporary special circumstances necessitated exceptional organisational forms. More cynical party members argued that the creation of national branches and committees allowed the British party to ignore work amongst national minorities. However the advocates of self-organisation—and the subsequent experience of unification backed them up—argued that the creation of national branches should be a recognition of not just of language but of cultural differences as well. In the cases of both the Cypriot and the West Indian branches, the failure to acknowledge and to tackle the cultural differences within the unified branches reinforced divisions between English and non-English members and contributed to the decline in membership. The possibility should not be discounted that many non-white or non-English party members experienced racism within party organisations as well as in the wider labour movement.

In the context of a communist party wedded to what in the 1950s was a narrow interpretation of class politics, national branches (except in cases of extreme language and cultural differences) were probably always an anomaly that acted to reinforce division rather than promote working class unity. However separate branches were not the only solutions to self-representation. Kuya points out the contradictions in allowing women's and youth sections within a party but not organisations based on nationality or ethnicity. She argues that it should be possible to work together on issues where there is common interest and in separate organisations for special interests. According to Carter, Billy Strachan believed that West Indian comrades should work in their party branches and in West Indian party organisations. In an interview with Mary Davis in 1982, Kay Beauchamp, who had been closely involved in relations between the London party and the national branches, expressed regret that these branches had been absorbed 'in favour of integration, which in practice hasn't been seen to work'.[38]

Membership of the basic party organisations along with a structure incorporating local 'national' groups, aggregate meetings and district/national committees with real influence on the party's decision-making process might have represented one possible solution. Certainly this structure might have prevented the isolation that many black or non-British comrades felt in the party and it may have acted as a counterbalance to the perceptions of institutional chauvinism and racism which affected the CPGB in the 1950s and 1960s. Such a structure, allied to a more positive attitude to issues of race and racism, might possibly have retained some of the members lost after the dissolution of the national branches. Instead of which, some of those who left the party went on to play a prominent role in the militant anti-racist and black power organisations of the 1960s and 1970s.

However, the impact of organisational changes was also determined by political considerations. Members of these branches were often much more interested in and swayed by international developments than were other British communists. Many of these comrades were primarily concerned with the struggles in the country or region of their origin and had joined the CPGB as the representative of the international communist movement rather than the party itself. In the context of the international developments of the period, particularly the Cuban revolution and Sino-Soviet split, this meant that the essentially pro-Soviet position of the British party would lead many members into conflict with the party. An interesting question here is the extent to which those Cypriot, West Indian or Indian party members who did remain within the CPGB had felt more incorporated within the British party than those who left.

The essence of the history of the national branches is that the CPGB tolerated and even encouraged their existence until they had clearly developed into alternative power structures within the party. Even under these circumstances, the party did not move to uphold its rules on organisation until it was clear that these structures were being used to attack or damage the party. In the context of the CPGB's stance on the disputes in the international communist movement, the party moved to close down a focus of internal dissent in the Indian branches. Moves for increased autonomy and dissent in the West Indian and Cypriot leadership probably also provoked central party action. The logic of democratic centralism meant that the CPGB had no mechanism to accommodate dissent and no way to support the evolution of democratic, federal structures within the party. For this reason, the national branches and the structures that had grown up around them had to be closed down.

Notes

1. Betty Matthews, London organiser, replying to the discussion of leading Cypriot members of the CPGB, 18 October 1966, CP/LON/ADVC/4/4, Communist Party Archive, National Museum of Labour History, Manchester (hereafter NMLH).
2. H. Adi, 'West Africans and the Communist Party in the 1950s', in G. Andrews, N. Fishman and K. Morgan (eds), *Opening the Books* (London, 1995); K. Newton, *The Sociology of British Communism* (London, 1969), p.78 has a brief reference to Cypriot organisation in the CPGB; R. Ramdin, *The Making of the Black Working Class in Britain* (London, 1987), p.400 refers to the existence of Indian branches and T. Carter, *Shattering Illusions* (London, 1986), pp.56–7 gives an account of the West Indian branches. See also M. Sherwood, *Claudia Jones* (London, 1999).
3. Papers relating to CPGB Committee on Party Organisation, 1965–6, CP/CENT/ORG/18/1 and CP/CENT/COMM/9/1–2, NMLH; CPGB Executive Committee minutes 22/23 May 1965, CP/CENT/EC/10/9, NMLH; J. Woddis to B. Moore, letter, 20 July 1966, CP/CENT/INT/38/01, NMLH; CPGB London district branch membership figures 1955–9, CP/CENT/ORG/19/5 and CP/CENT/DISC R. Ballin file, NMLH.
4. D. Kuya, CPGB biographical project, interview with Andrew Flinn, 26 January 2000; Carter, *Illusions*, p.57; R. P. Dutt's notes for CPGB Political Committee, 29 November 1963, CP/CENT/DISC A. Manchanda file, NMLH.
5. 'The future work of Cypriot communists in London', 28 April 1966, CP/LON/ADVC/4/4, NMLH.
6. CP/CENT/DISC E. Joannides file, 24 January and 26 February 1953, NMLH. Joannides left Cyprus after being expelled from university for political activity and joined the CPGB in 1930. A writer and journalist, he was one of the leading

British Cypriot comrades in the 1930s, 1940s and 1950s.
7. 'The future work'; Joannides file, 30 January and 9 April 1953; CPGB London district membership figures, CP/CENT/ORG/19/3–5, NMLH; 5th Conference of Cypriot branches of CPGB, 19–20 June 1965, CP/LON/ADVC/4/2, NMLH; undated note on Cypriot membership outside London, CP/LON/ADVC/4/9, NMLH. By 1966 Cypriot branches were to found in most areas of Greater London but the largest memberships were in the boroughs of Camden, Islington and Haringey, CP/LON/ORG/2/10, NMLH. In 1966 total London party membership was 7,036.
8. 4th Conference of Cypriot branches of CPGB, CP/LON/ADVC/4/8, NMLH; 5th Conference, CP/LON/ADVC/4/2.
9. 'The future work'; a similarly titled document, n.d., CP/LON/ADVC/4/8, NMLH; G. McLennan to J. Woddis, letter, 22 February 1966, CP/LON/ADVC/4/9, NMLH.
10. 'The future work'; a similarly titled document, CP/LON/ADVC/4/8; report of a meeting of sixteen leading Cypriot comrades, 18 October 1966, CP/LON/ADVC/4/4, NMLH; 'The first year of unification', 28 June 1967, CP/LON/ADVC/4/5, NMLH; Cypriot Advisory Committee minutes 10 July 1968, CP/LONADVC/4/6, NMLH; 'Draft points on the problem of Cypriot members', April 1970, CP/LON/ADC/4/7, NMLH.
11. 'Draft points'; list of London Cypriot members, 1980, CP/LON/ADVC/5/1, NMLH. Cypriot membership fell by over 80 per cent over 15 years while the decline in district and national membership was closer to 50 per cent, CP/CENT/ORG/19/3–4, NMLH.
12. 'Report on progress of Cypriot integration', 9 August 1966, CP/LON/ADVC/4/4, NMLH.
13. 'Report on progress'; 'The first year'; 'Some borough reports on the position of Cypriot unification', 1967, CP/LON/ADVC/4/5, NMLH; A. Kleanthous to F. Stanley, letter, 16 February 1970, CP/LON/ADVC/4/10, NMLH.
14. 'The first year'; Cypriot Advisory Committee; M. Egelnick notes re. CPGB and the Cypriot community, 27 January 1986 CP/LON/ADVC/5/8, NMLH; Kleanthous to Stanley, letter.
15. 'The first year'; Cypriot Advisory Committee.
16. Cypriot Advisory Committee; Cypriot Advisory Committee minutes 20 September 1968, CP/LON/ORG/3/1, NMLH; 'Cypriot unification', 5 June 1968, CP/LON/ADVC/4/6, NMLH; 'Proposals for changes in the organisation at borough and branch level for Cypriot comrades', 10 April 1969, CP/LON/ADVC/4/6, NMLH; 'Problems of Cypriot membership', September 1970, CP/LON/ADVC/4/8, NMLH; F. Stanley to R. Falber, letter, 25 September 1970; CPGB Political Committee March 1971; London District Committee minutes 17 September 1972, all CP/LON/ADVC/4/10, NMLH.
17. Cypriot Advisory Committee 1968; H. Mitchell, 'Draft statement to conference on the question of unification', 6 June 1971, CP/LON/ADVC/4/12, NMLH;

Kleanthous to Stanley, letter.
18. Cypriot Advisory Committee 1968; 'Draft points on the problem of Cypriot members', March 1970, CP/LON/ADVC/4/7, NMLH; 'Problems of Cypriot Membership'.
19. 'Draft on work of party members on UCB committees', n.d., CP/LON/ADVC/4/9, NMLH; 'Draft points'; CP/CENT/DISC Hatjiepieris file. Evdoros Joannides and Evagoras Economides were among a number of comrades who in 1953 came into bitter conflict with Pefkos and were suspended from the CPGB over their alleged support for an expelled faction in AKEL. George Hatjiepieris was suspended from the Cypriot branches and subsequently refused readmission to the party, in part because of his criticism of AKEL's support for Archbishop Makarios.
20. Kleanthous to Stanley, letter.
21. Ramdin, *Black Working Class*, pp.396–7; P. Fryer, *Staying Power. The history of Black people in Britain* (London, 1989), pp.372–5; CP/BIOG V. Sharma file; Manchanda file; *Report on Midlands Youth*, 14 May 1956, CP/CENT/ORG/5/2, NMLH.
22. J. Woddis, draft of presentation to special meeting of leading Indian party members and district representatives, 13 February 1966; 'Indian party members of the CPGB', 25 October 1966, CP/CENT/INT/38/01, NMLH.
23. 'Indian party members'; Ramdin, Black Working Class, p.400; V. Sharma EC nomination, CP/CENT/CONG/13/2, NMLH; J. Gollan to A. Manchanda, letter, 15 January 1964, Manchanda file.
24. 'Indian party members'; Ramdin, *Black Working Class*, pp.402–7; Sharma file; Manchanda file; CP/CENT/DISC R. Singh file, NMLH; CP/CENT/DISC S.S. Sandhu and J. Joshi file, NMLH. Sherwood, *Jones*, pp.50–1 gives an account of Manchanda's somewhat abrasive and sectarian politics and his antagonistic relationship with the CPGB.
25. 'Indian party members'; Ramdin, *Black Working Class*, Sharma file; Sandhu and Joshi file.
26. Manchanda file; I. Cox to J. Woddis, letter, 16 May 1966, CP/CENT/INT/38/01, NMLH.
27. Woddis, draft of presentation...; 'Indian party members'; 'Information document on Indian members of the CPGB and organisation questions', CP/CENT/INT/38/01, NMLH.
28. 'Indian party members'; J. Woddis to H. Bourne, letter, 17 February 1966; B. Moore to J. Woddis, letter, 15 July 1966; Resignations 18 September 1966 and 3 March 1967; 'Indian members of the CPGB', 23 February 1976; Report by V. Sharma on activities of Indian comrades, 21 December 1988, all CP/CENT/INT/38/01, NMLH; Manchanda file.
29. Carter, *Illusions*, pp.56–7; Carter, 2000; Cleston Taylor, CPGB biographical project, interview by Mike Squires, 1999; Chris Le Maitre, CPGB biographical project, interview by Mike Squires, 2000; CPGB West Indian Committee file, CP/CENT/CTTE/2/4, NMLH; Sherwood, *Jones*, pp.68–9.

30. LDCP membership returns 1955, CP/CENT/ORG/19/5, NMLH; Sherwood, *Jones*; Carter 2000; Taylor, 2000; CP/CENT/DISC J. James file 1963, NMLH; CPGB Race Relations Committee, CP/CENT/CTTE/2/5–7, NMLH; Kuya, 2000.
31. Carter, Illusions, pp.56, 60–1; 'West Indians in Britain', IAC 1957, CP/CENT/CTTE/2/4, NMLH.
32. Kuya, 2000; Sherwood, *Jones*.
33. Copies of *British Road to Socialism* as published and revised 1951, 1957 and 1958; papers from Commissions on the BRS, CP/CENT/COMM/1/1–3, NMLH; Carter, *Illusions*, pp.59–60, CP/CENT/DISC R. Chandrisingh file, NMLH; Le Maitre, 2000; CPGB West Indian Committee submission to BRS Commission, 1 October 1956, CP/CENT/COMM/1/5, NMLH; S.Howe, *Anticolonialism in British Politics* (Oxford, 1993), pp.297–9, Sherwood, *Jones*, pp.63–4; Kuya, 2000.
34. Carter, *Illusions*, p.56; Carter, 2000; Le Maitre, 2000; Taylor, 1999; P. Jeffrey, CPGB biographical project, interview by Mike Squires, 2000.
35. Carter, *Illusions*, pp.57–61; Carter, 2000; CP/CENT/DISC F. Bailey, NMLH; report on activities of Victor Blyth, CP/CENT/ORG/21/1, NMLH.
36. James file; CP/CENT/DISC Stoke Newington branch file and Howe, *Anticolonialism*, pp.292–3.
37. Carter, *Illusions*, pp.61–2, 150; Taylor 1999.
38. Carter 2000; Kuya 2000; Beauchamp in *Link*, spring 1982, p.11.

Communists are not Born, they are Made
The political education system of the French Communist Party

Marja Kivisaari

> We must say not only to the Russians, but also to foreigners that the most important thing in the period now beginning is to learn. We do learn, in a general way; they will have to learn, in a special way, in order to really understand the organisation, structure, methods, and nature of revolutionary work. If this is done, I am certain that prospects for worldwide revolution will be not only good but excellent.
>
> *V. I. Lenin*[1]

This article examines how the influence of the centrally controlled and directed political education of successive generations of party cadres, in Stalin's words 'people of a special mould', reinforced the authority and power of the leadership of the French Communist Party [PCF]. It argues that by the skilful utilisation of the party's organisational principle, democratic centralism, and by the systematic use of its political training system the successive communist leaderships ensured the availability of politically committed and ideologically sound cadres who would perpetuate the conservative outlook of their superiors and thus secure their authority and power.

The historical origins and development of the PCF's political education system from its foundation to 1990 provide a useful point of departure and a backdrop for the study. This then proceeds to a brief discussion of the PCF's organisational principle of democratic centralism and, in particular, its reality and practice as a tool of the communist leadership. Finally, we shall conclude with an assessment of the role of the communist political education system as the key element in the preservation of the leadership's authority and power.

The origins and early development

The French Communist Party was born at the Congress of Tours in December 1920, when the majority of the delegates of the French Socialist

Party voted to join the Third or Communist International (Comintern). The PCF's educational work goes back to the very beginning of the party's existence, and the first permanent party schools at regional and central level were set up under the Comintern's supervision at the beginning of the bolshevisation process in 1924.[2] Until the mid-1930s, however, much of the formal higher political training of the French communist leaders took place in the International Lenin School in Moscow which had been officially opened in 1926.[3] Subjects studied at the school included Marxist political economy, history of the labour movement, history and structures of the Soviet party and the Russian language. Theoretical studies of Marxism-Leninism were not however the only reason for the students to be sent to Moscow: they also went there to be tested and selected for their subsequent party careers. Students were also trained in organisational methods, infiltration techniques and all aspects of clandestine work.[4]

It was not until the PCF made the critical transition to a mass-based political party in the Popular Front era that the French party leadership came to fully understand the value and importance of an efficient political education system to satisfy the party's urgent need for trained militants. In 1932 the PCF's Seventh Congress voted through a special resolution detailing an ambitious training programme operating on three levels (elementary, regional and central) which Etienne Fajon, the 'Father' of the PCF's political education system, was appointed to oversee. By the end of the 1930s, the reorganised political training system was providing a solid basis and a sound framework for the training of large numbers of militants and cadres who flocked to the party during the Popular Front, when party membership rose from 87,000 (1935) to 319,000 (1938). It should also be noted that already, coupled with the PCF's organisational principle of democratic centralism, the party education system was being developed into an excellent tool for preserving the pre-eminence and authority of party leader Maurice Thorez's working-class leadership group, or *groupe dirigeant fondamental*, which had resulted from the successful implementation of the bolshevisation programme in the PCF.[5] The 'total school experience' was thus on its way to moulding students into loyal activists who, in their turn, would provide trustworthy, predominantly working-class leadership material for the party and its mass organisations.

The PCF entered the immediate post-war period as the dominant force in French politics, with new responsibilities, both at national and local level, which required ideologically correct leadership skills and a far greater degree of organisational cohesion than hitherto. The party also needed reliable functionaries to operate the vast internal apparatus that was being built up, and trained cadres to direct its mass mobilisation work. The massive growth of the membership, which passed 800,000 members in 1946, also meant that most new members lacked both theoretical knowledge and practical experience. During the Occupation, no organised political education had been provided, and the party school network painstakingly built up by Etienne Fajon had perished completely. Despite the remaining hard core of fully indoctrinated and dedicated militants, there was a shortage of trained instructors at all levels due to so many leading cadres having lost their lives during the war. Upon his return from Algiers, where he had spent the war, the indefatigable Fajon relaunched the party's political training programme, and by the 1950s, the PCF's network of schools was again operating vigorously at all three levels.[6]

The study programmes were drawn up by the Education Sector.[7] As the schools were not 'schools' in the traditional sense of the word, there were very few subjects per se, and Marxist philosophy, political economy and history were central themes common to all eras. Instead, the teaching tended to focus on various traditional or topical *thèmes* relevant to a particular period. The *thèmes* were generally based on the resolutions and decisions of the party congresses and accurately reflected the changes and shifts of party policy as determined by political circumstances and developments in France and abroad—usually the Soviet Union—at any given time. A good illustration of the way in which a major shift was presented in the study programmes is provided by the teaching of contemporary history in the aftermath of the Khrushchev report in 1956. On Thorez's instructions, the notorious *Précis d'histoire du Parti bolchévik* or *History of the CPSU (B) (Short course)* was not to be relied upon as before but rather 'treated with caution'. From now on, he wrote, 'for the French Party, the essential thing is the history of the French labour movement and it is around this history that we must organize our study'.[8]

In the Cold War climate, then, the political education system already presented in many ways a mirror image of the party. Like the PCF, it too appeared successful, enthusiastic and dynamic in the immediate post-war era; and just like the PCF, isolated from mainstream politics in France, the political education system then threw itself into the feverish counter-community life style in order to help preserve communist identity and values in the hostile environment. In this activity it proved its worth by maintaining the morale and motivation of party members, militants and cadres and by acting as an invaluable mechanism for safeguarding the leadership's authority, even when that leadership was physically absent, as Maurice Thorez was in the early 1950s.

Soviet influence remained strong in the PCF's political education system well into the 1970s and an important number of the major figures in the party were trained in Moscow. The selection process was supervised by both the PCF and the CPSU to ensure that only 'trustworthy' people were sent.[9] The students' expenses were met by the CPSU and they lived in an *internat* with a huge library, sports centre, cinema, billiard room, and other facilities which emphasised their privileged, if isolated, status. As in the 1930s, the schooling period served a dual function of inculcating theory and assessing the communist personality. It is a testimony to their unshakeable loyalty and the efficacy of the training process that even after encountering the Soviet reality, most students remained faithful to their ideals.

Cautious changes in the PCF, as first advocated by Waldeck Rochet's leadership in the 1960s, were also reflected in the political education programmes as they introduced the concept of a Common Programme to the trainee cadres and guided them on the path towards the Union of the Left (the *Union de la Gauche*, formed between the PCF and the French Socialist Party in 1972). This was followed by attempts to change the rigid methods of teaching by allowing more open debate and free discussion; again, this mirrored the PCF's efforts towards greater openness and flexibility in the early 1970s. Ironically, the PCF's new strategy of alliance building and openness made the education system's traditional role as a reinforcer of party identity somewhat redundant in the early days of the Union of the Left. However, this function was quickly reactivated when, after the break-up in 1979 of the Union of the Left, the communist leadership returned to isolation and its policy of *centralité ouvrière*, i.e the belief that the working class should play a central and dominant role in society and politics. This policy was reflected in the social origins of the central schools' student population, in particular those of the PCF's elite four-month central schools, where students from working-class backgrounds dominated, providing very nearly half of the schools' student population between 1974 and 1980.[10] The students' sociological composition was in fact a mirror image of the party's top leadership structure in which workers represented half (49.6 per cent) of all members of the Central Committee in 1976.[11] On the other hand, coupled with the rise of the middle class, this period also saw the emergence of a new type of student and party member, better educated and better informed than in the past, who now began to express criticism of the 'simplistic' study programmes and methods used in party schools. This new development was in clear conflict with the 'reproletarianisation' programme which the communist leadership, by systematically favouring the access of working-class students to the higher echelons of the party, was preparing to implement at the precise time when the working class in France was diminishing significantly. Thus, despite developments outside of the party and efforts made at party modernisation which called for a more differentiated leadership, the PCF's leadership model at the highest echelon remained resolutely stuck in the past and ill equipped for the challenges of the 1980s.

Throughout the 1980s the PCF found itself in a situation of accelerated and unrelenting decline. As the leadership controlled the preparation of the study programmes, the incoherent and vague strategies which were prompted by the party's needs to survive were conveyed to the dwindling student audience in party schools.[12] While the training system had previously proved a useful means of introducing, updating and maintaining the party's strategic choices, it now had nothing coherent to convey. The hastily prepared study programmes were merely responses to the slogans issued by the party congresses and the Marchais leadership and lacked inspiration and intellectual vision. With the membership in decline—from 520,000 in 1978 to 330,000 in 1987—militancy on the wane, and student numbers less than half of those in the previous decade, the whole relevance of the education system seemed in doubt.[13] The final blow came with the collapse of communism; this was the last chance for the party and the education system which it controlled, to engage in self-criticism, and to respond in a new manner. The party would not, and the education system therefore could not; both thus continued to perpetuate the inflexibility, immobilism and conservatism that had been their trademarks for much of their existence, still propping up the authority and disproportionate power of the sclerotic party leadership.

Democratic centralism and the leadership

Before examining the factors which made the PCF's political education system so vitally important for the preservation of the leadership's authority and power, we need to take a brief look at the party's organisational principle of democratic centralism. Based on the PCF's revolutionary theory, democratic centralism was the condition for the ideological and political cohesion of the party, and for its unity of action. The main principles were free discussion at all levels; majority decisions applied by all; interdiction of all fractional activity; democratic election of leading organs of the various levels of the party; collective leadership; accountability of elected leading bodies to their electors; the decisions of higher organs to be binding on lower organs to ensure the strength of the party; and finally, freely exercised criticism and self-criticism in all organisations and at all levels of the party.[14] On the face of it, there is nothing special in the *theory* of democratic centralism as defined by the rules of the PCF that would set it apart from the rules and regulations of other parties. But as observers generally point out, the *theoretical definition* does not reflect the reality and practice of democratic centralism. This is supported by Georges Marchais' own words during the preparations for the PCF's 25th congress in 1984: 'Democratic centralism fits on a postage stamp; all that matters is how it is practised.'[15] Therefore, democratic centralism should be examined through the eyes of its critics in order to interpret what the party rules leave unsaid—what Georges Lavau calls *le non-dit*—rather than what they do say.

The leadership in fact had a battery of weapons at its disposal for 'practising' democratic centralism and controlling intra-party debate. The 'unhealthy' aspects, the 'six sins' (*péchés*) of democratic centralism have been spelled out with particular clarity by Michel Naudy, a journalist and a former PCF member.[16] First, only the outgoing leadership had the right to draw up the pre-congress draft resolution (no alternatives were allowed) which the Politbureau then more or less rubberstamped. Second, the leadership controlled the party's main organ, *L'Humanité*, the platform for all 'open' discussion and the only 'legal' means of diffusing the thoughts and proposals of party members to all communists. Third, the leadership was able to direct and control the progress of the debate by applying the principle of 'collective leadership' in respect of outgoing leaders during the preparatory stages of the party congress. Fourth, the leadership's line was the official line and the only one that got voiced. Only the representatives of the leadership had access to party media; this enabled the leadership to intervene from outside any debate and subtly direct the course of the debate. Fifth, the leadership had complete knowledge of everything that took place within the party due to the vertical structure of the communist party. The base of the communist pyramid was formed by cells where freedom of discussion was traditionally almost total; but the cells were isolated and there was no horizontal cell network across the country. Consequently, the only communication was from the base up (whereas the discipline flowed from top down). Finally, the leadership had at its disposal an 'elite army' of paid party workers, the so-called *permanents* most of whom had *been trained in party schools*. The *permanents* were an important cog in the machinery of democratic centralism and much has been written about them, their devotion to the cause and their unwavering loyalty.[17] For the purposes of applying the principle of democratic centralism, the *permanents* occupied diverse functions and had different levels of status. The eminent historians of French communism Annie Kriegel and Georges Lavau have both defined them as *politically trained* men and women who had abandoned—for good, in most cases—their original occupations, and who depended on the party, directly or indirectly, for their income, career prospects, standard of life and promotion.

The pyramidal structure was repeated in the way that cadres were appointed: all leaders, however modest their function, were designated by the next level above them and the lower level generally only confirmed the decision. Moreover, before being able to enter the Politbureau, a candidate had to be elected right through the system—cell, section, federation, party congress and finally Central Committee—and also had to be included in the majority group which alone could 'supply' delegates. Consequently, a handful of people at the top was able to decide about everything, having confiscated all means of debate. Fittingly, Naudy writes that 'from democratic centralism, the PCF moved to aristocratic centralism'.[18] In this way, the leadership became a sinecure for a small co-opted elite whose word was law and who applied its own brand of democratic centralism in order to resist challenges to its authority or orthodoxy—and to perpetuate itself.

The general validity of the criticism expressed by communist party dissidents—that the system, by its operation and practices, made it difficult to propose and implement change—is therefore confirmed, and the party leadership is shown to have been able to make use of the organisational principle of democratic centralism in order to retain its disproportionate power. This prompts the question of why and how the communist leadership was able to implement this principle—which seemed in theory to be highly democratic—in such an undemocratic way. The answer is simple: it had at its disposal a trained body of functionaries and militants who would unquestioningly apply party policy and thwart any attempt to oppose it. Therefore, while democratic centralism formed the infrastructure and framework for the way the party functioned, it was only permitted to do so within the context of the communist theory and ideology which acted as the 'cement' or discipline holding the party together. Since the discipline of a communist party relies heavily on the conviction and commitment of its members, it is evident that their loyalty to the party would not develop to the necessary degree without a systematic strengthening of their grasp of party theory and ideology. Theory and ideology therefore had to be taught. Thus, by dovetailing the functions of democratic centralism and political education, the leadership succeeded in adroitly securing all the power in its own hands and thus ensured its own succession by ideologically reliable cadres.

In the final section of this study we shall focus on the importance of the PCF's political education system as the *key element* which gave the definitive refining touch to the moulding process of a select body of people destined for special functions and higher responsibilities within the party and its mass organisations. These were the ideologically sound militants and cadres who would perpetuate the conservative outlook of their superiors and thus secure their authority and power.

Political education as the key element

Where communist parties enjoyed a political monopoly, everyone was subject to ideological education in schools, the media and culture and the workplace. At the same time, there was a separate and specific system of party schooling for party members and functionaries. However, in non-communist countries the agencies of socialisation are under state control and that of other social forces. The communist parties therefore developed their own socialisation programme for members and ancillary organisations to counter the wider cultural and political hegemonic discourse. This generated an alternative subculture or counterculture.[19] New recruits had in most cases already been exposed to a number of other agents of political socialisation. One was the family—'I was born with communist blood in my veins', said one respondent—or what Lavau calls membership by immersion (*'l'adhésion d'imprégnation'*).[20] Others were peer groups, the school or workplace, a student or a communist youth organisation, or a trade union. Joining the party was thus often regarded as a logical next step taking a person's political commitment one degree further.[21] The party then continued the process of purposive political socialisation by disseminating information, organising debates, enabling its members to understand politics and express their opinions, and—in the case of a select body of people—by providing them with a theoretical and practical political education programme in party-run training schools.[22]

The Soviet system of party schools was thus mirrored in communist parties in Western democracies and political education—in general terms, the 'inculcation of and identification with the goals and values of a political community'[23]—therefore formed an important part of the socialising process of the party activist. In addition, political education also constituted a method by which political recruitment into specific roles in the party and its various organisations was effected.

In western democracies communist parties traditionally recruited mainly from the most disadvantaged social categories for whom the party functioned as 'an important and even irreplaceable agent of political socialisation', compensating for their social, educational and cultural handicaps.[24] This was particularly important in the case of the French Communist Party: first, because the majority of PCF activists came from the lower social classes; and second, because the party's 'particular and rigid world view' (Marxism-Leninism) had to be taught in order to maintain ideological unity between the Communism of the intellectuals and the Communism of the rank-and-file militants'.[25] Through political education, the PCF sought to control both groups. In the case of the former, the leadership had to ensure that the ability of the intellectuals to innovate and criticise would remain within the limits set by the official party line.[26] According to a former PCF member, a good communist leader needs 'enough intelligence to take the initiative in the carrying-out of orders, but not enough intelligence to question those orders'.[27] As for the militants, they had to be provided with political training which would enable them to integrate the political and cultural world of communism and help them internalise the objectives of the party.[28]

The element of 'continuity' (that is to say, the training schools as a continuing aspect of the daily processes of the political education of a cadre) was the leitmotiv running through the communist pedagogy. The fact that communist theory was being constantly applied and tested in action meant that the communist had to be continually studying and learning. The concept of the 'unity of theory and practice' also demanded that there be no separation between training and party life. In communist party practice every activity had some pedagogical value, be it reading or selling the party press, attending meetings, participating in campaigns, demonstrations or strikes, and so on. The party schools were therefore not intended to be divorced from the general process of moulding cadres but rather to complete this process. Their importance lay in the fact that in that process they occupied key points, 'nodes of intense development'.[29] Kriegel emphasises that 'these schools were not centres for the formulation of doctrine or for research'; they were intended purely 'for the cadres, unswervingly dedicated to the training of political leaders needed by the party', to mould professionals, or in the Leninist sense of the term, 'professional revolutionaries'.[30]

A measure of the high importance attached to the training schools is demonstrated by the way in which the students were selected. The selection process was carried out directly by the leading committees of the party echelon immediately below that on which the training school was to be conducted; and the ratification (or rejection) of nominations was decided by the leading organs of the echelon at whose level the school was organised.[31] Kriegel underlines the fact that the students 'were not volunteers'.[32] According to Marcel Rosette, who directed the PCF's central schools in 1956–63, at a given point during their party career, 'promising' militants were simply 'told to do the schools'.[33] The suitable candidates had already been socialised into the party and their recruitment to party schools was based on the manifestation of leadership capacity and considerable experience in organisational work. A working-class background, trade union work, preferably in a large enterprise, and elective mandates were also important in the selection process. The fact that the students could not 'just volunteer' for party training did not mean that they were without motivation—quite the opposite. Predominantly, 'going to school' was considered as a 'mission', an honour and a responsibility.[34] During their period of political training, the students also expected to learn more about the party and Marxism to help them in the 'fight against social injustice and poverty', and to gain personal goals in the field of self-development.[35] Political education was not seen 'officially' as an avenue to a career since 'careerism' and 'promotion' were considered as dirty words.[36]

For all that, attendance in party schools offered distinct rewards. As Offerlé puts it, if the division of political work often seems to the outsider 'a complete domination by the leaders of the led'(*une domination sans partage des dirigeants sur les dirigés*), it is possible only because those who are dominated are satisfied with the advantages they are drawing from the situation.[37] For most students, participation in party training schools opened up opportunities which were more satisfactory than those that were available outside. In many ways, trained militants had a chance to succeed socially on the basis of 'unconventional' criteria which required no particular technical proficiency or scholarly attainment. As a large proportion of the students came from a working-class background, many of them came to owe their entire political, educational and cultural progress to the party and its teachings.[38] In socio-cultural terms, 'quitting production' and becoming a party functionary, a 'militant penpusher' or an 'activist hacking at the coalface of history', frequently meant a new life dedicated to previously unknown intellectual activities: reading, writing, discussion, a 'life enriched and stimulated by people and events'.[39] These were the functionaries who were the crucial cogs in the machinery of democratic centralism. In return for their material security, they accepted the need for conformism, ideological prudence and unwavering loyalty to the party.[40] In the words of Duverger, their existence had created 'a bureaucracy, an oligarchy…which exercised power, retained it and transmitted it by means of co-option'.[41]

In the French Communist Party, the bureaucratic oligarchy assumed the form of 'technocratic oligarchy' which meant that in principle, the courses organised for the party cadre had to be attended before they could expect a post of leadership. Interviews with the PCF's former education chiefs and central school directors (Etienne Fajon, Francette Lazard, Marcel Rosette, Charles Fiterman, Nicholas Pasquarelli, Henri Martin, Jean-François Rivière and Lucien Bossu) established that attendance in party schools undoubtedly contributed to progress in the party. Indeed, for certain cadre levels (naturally including that of the PCF's central school directors) it was a strict requirement and Fajon, who headed the PCF's Education Sector in 1935–48 and 1974–79, wrote in his autobiography: 'I don't know a single party leader, at the federal level or higher, who has not benefited from their political education at some time or other.'[42] This was also confirmed by all former students who were interviewed: each stage of their schooling coincided with a move to a more responsible or higher position. According to Lavabre, who has researched the cadre profiles of the Paris Federation, then the PCF's largest, during the period 1965–77, the more important the federation, the more rigorous was the training of cadres: 'Attending party schools is the rule.'[43] In 1977, only 15 per cent of the federal cadres in Paris had *not* attended a party school at central level, and Elleinstein records that out of the 1522 delegates who participated in the PCF's 22nd Congress in 1976, only 283 had not attended any party training school.[44]

Unlike other types of parties such as 'parties of elites' or 'parties of patronage', mass parties or 'parties of militants' have rarely been in a position to reward their collaborators in financial terms or by means of patronage, and have therefore had to develop other types of rewards in order to retain their support.[45] Thus, the rigid organisational hierarchy of the Communist Party was in fact a pre-requisite for the system of rewards of a mass party such as the PCF became in the mid-1930s. Gaxie points out that one of the notable characteristics of these parties is the proliferation of their closely-linked hierarchic echelons.[46] Indeed, in his report to the PCF's 16th Congress Georges Marchais claimed that '...[with our] thirty thousand members responsible for cells, 25 000 section leaders, 3300 federal leaders, with our 1400 mayors, 21 000 municipal councillors and 150 departmental councillors...with our tens of thousands of communists responsible for mass organisations and movements, we have cadres totalling more than 100 000!'[47] In the Communist Party, the possibility of advancement therefore essentially played the same role as does the social mobility of the elite in society; militancy reinforced with theoretical training thus offered an even more effective channel for self-realisation.[48] To this must be added that the nature of the rewards could also be merely symbolic and psychological (affection, admiration, prestige), sometimes just a matter of being able to quench one's 'thirst to learn'—a theme that would recur time and time over again in the personal testimonies of former teachers and students of the PCF training schools.[49]

During the learning period, then, through cognitive and affective processes the student was expected to gradually internalise as his 'own' the party's political norms. The teaching about the party's history, its heroes, its traditions and its contributions to the nation and the country further enhanced the student's partisan pride and identity.[50] This and the reading of carefully prescribed popular literature (Soviet novels, short stories and reportage of Soviet life as well as films) not only fostered emotional links between the students themselves but also between them and their 'heroic and glorious Soviet comrades' and the entire international communist family.[51] The very real physical isolation from home and family during the prolonged study period (one to six months in France, up to two years in the Soviet Union) was compensated by the fraternal atmosphere of the training establishments. The 'total school experience'—lectures, classes, group debates and discussions, personal study periods, the communal meals and celebrations, periods of 'organised relaxation' and sports, excursions, practical work sessions, relations between students and instructors, and so on—was a carefully planned exercise, the purpose of which was the reinforcement of the students' emotional attachment to each other and to the party. The training schools in fact reproduced a miniature version of the communist counter-community where a small group of people, put together for a specific purpose 'bonded' and formed strong (sometimes life-long) attachments.

Thus, the students became politically socialised not only through the deliberate orientation of the teaching dispensed, but also through their entire holistic learning experience. It is obvious that acquisition of earlier political socialisation on the emotional level had already acted as a suitable springboard for what was a further enhancement in the form of specific political training for carefully selected people. The subsequent formal instruction provided to a 'chosen' group of people by the party schools was the final piece in the jigsaw that made up the fully trained and politically socialised cadre. The result was a closed, well disciplined, mechanised and monolithic party organization; one which resembled a military apparatus, but whose methods of regimentation and control were considerably more adaptable and efficient because they were based on *a training of minds* rather than that of bodies. It was this training that claimed to provide a complete and final philosophy of the universe and whose aim was to preserve communist identity and unity, and to secure and reinforce the power and authority of the leadership which rested on that identity and unity. The importance of the PCF's training procedures in transforming a heterogeneous assortment of party activists into a coherent political force, 'people of a special mould', and in producing committed, ideologically correct leaders is therefore unquestionable, and the issue of how the PCF trained its leadership thus becomes pivotal to the understanding of the party's history and evolution.

Notes

1. Lenin's speech to the Fourth Congress of the Communist International, 15 November 1922; cited in A. Kriegel, *The French Communists: Profile of a People* (Chicago, 1972), p.254.
2. For an excellent account of the early years of the PCF's political education, see Danielle Tartakowsky, *Ecoles et Editions communistes 1921–33* (Thèse pour le Doctorat de 3e cycle, Université de Paris VIII, 1977).
3. Branko Lazitch, 'La formation des cadres dirigeants', *Pouvoirs*, no. 21 (1982), p.41. Many former ILS students later became leaders of their respective national parties. Waldeck Rochet, Gus Hall, Josip Broz Tito, Wladyslaw Gomulka and Ville Pessi all attended the International Lenin School.
4. Marja Van Digglen (now Kivisaari), 'Communist Party Education in Finland: from Red Flags to Wine Tasting', *Journal of Communist Studies*, vol. 7, no. 4 (1991), p.489.
5. See Bernard Pudal, *Prendre partie: pour une sociologie historique du Parti communiste français*. (Paris, 1989). Pudal also examines certain aspects of the PCF's political education system in the 1930s.
6. Marcel Rosette, the future communist mayor, senator and member of the Central Committee, who was to direct the Party's central schools in 1956–63, paints a vivid picture of the resumption of training activities in the immediate postwar period: 'Cadres could not be trained solely on the basis of everyday experience—they needed theoretical "baggage". They simply had to go to the schools—at that time, the question was not even asked! I mean, it was just normal to go to a party school! Completely normal! ... In my case, as soon as the war had ended, I was attending an elementary school in my village [near Bourg-en-Bresse]. There were 360 inhabitants and we were all members of a cell. We went to the school, we attended the lessons, we had brochures; we attended school during five consecutive weeks. Somebody presented the brochures and the lessons; there were discussions. There were workers, farm workers, and in all France, it was like that! Oh yes!' (Interview with Marcel Rosette 9 September 1991.)
7. Interview with Henri Martin (central school director 1978–83), 31 March 1992.
8. Maurice Thorez, 'L'enseignment du marxisme-léninisme dans les écoles du Parti', *Cahiers du communisme*, no. 11, November 1956, pp.1202–7.
9. Interviews with Nicholas Pasquarelli (central school director 1962–6) 9 September 1991 and Guy Poussy (student in Moscow 1962–3) 9 July 1992.
10. Marja Kivisaari, 'The Decline of the French Communist Party: the party education system as a brake to change 1945–90'. (Portsmouth, PhD, 2000), pp.173–8. The precise figure was 47.8 per cent.
11. Marc Lazar, *Maisons rouges*. (Paris, 1992), p.248.
12. Stident numbers in both the one and four-month central schools dropped by almost 50 per cent in the period 1981–90. See Kivisaari, 'Decline', pp.200–5.
13. Membership figures from Stephane Courtois and Marc Lazar, *Histoire du Parti*

communiste français (Paris, 1995), p.423; see also S. Hazareesingh, *Intellectuals and the French Communist Party: disillusion and decline* (Oxford, 1991), p.8.
14. M. Waller, 'Democratic Centralism: the costs of discipline', in M. Waller and M. Fennema (eds.), *Communist Parties in Western Europe* (Oxford, 1988), pp.264–5.
15. M. Naudy, *PCF: le suicide* (Paris, 1986), p.109.
16. Naudy, *PCF*, pp.109–19.
17. See in particular Kriegel, *French Communists*; Georges Lavau, *A quoi sert le PCF?* (Paris, 1981).
18. Naudy, *PCF*, p.119.
19. See in particular Kriegel, *French Communists*.
20. Lavau, *A quoi sert le PCF?*, p.104. See also J. Derville and M. Croisat, 'La socialisation des militants communistes français: éléments d'une enquête dans l'Isére', *Revue française de science politique*, vol. XXIX, août, 1979, p.766. Derville and Croisat state that 66.3 per cent of the new party members in their study came from a left-wing family (communist or non-communist) with 46 per cent having at least one member of the family in the PCF.
21. On reasons why people join the Communist Party, see G. Almond, *The Appeals of Communism* (Princeton, New Jersey, 1956), p.224; and D. Gaxie, 'Economie des partis et rétributions du militantisme', *Revue française de science politique*, (1977) pp.143–7.
22. Derville and Croisat, 'La socialisation', p.760.
23. E. Propper Mickiewicz, *Soviet Political Schools. The Communist Party Adult Education System* (New Haven and London, 1967), p.1.
24. D. Gaxie, *Le cens caché* (Paris, 1978), p.180.
25. Derville and Croisat, 'La socialisation', p.761. Here the authors quote Gramsci's analysis of the role of the Jesuits who attempted to prevent a community dividing into two groups, 'that of the intellectuals and that of the simple souls'.
26. *Ibid*. This was done by 'sanctioning doctrinal evolutions and bringing them in line with orthodoxy'. See F. Bon, 'Structure de l'idéologie communiste', in *Le communisme en France* (Paris, 1969), p.136.
27. Almond, *Appeals*, p.139.
28. Derville and Croisat, 'La socialisation', p.761.
29. F. Meyer, *The Moulding of Communists. The training of a communist cadre.* (New York, 1961), p.162.
30. Kriegel, *French Communists*, pp.259–62.
31. Thus, in the case of the PCF, students for the federal school were proposed by the cell or section committees and ratified by responsible federal bureaux. Students for the central schools were nominated by federal committees and ratified by the Central Committee. Students for international schools in the USSR were selected by the Politbureau and ratified by the CPSU.
32. Kriegel, *French Communists*, p.264. Kriegel adds: 'Had they been [volunteers], the schools would have been filled with worthy individuals but who nonetheless were not the right kind of people for the kind of work the schools were designed to perform.'

33. Interview with Marcel Rosette 9 September 1991. In 1951, the Seine federation of the PCF sent the following letter to its section secretaries, members of the federal committee and political education chiefs: 'The Federal Secretariat has decided that three schools should be held during the holiday period. [...] We would ask you: 1) to send us, quickly, to the Federation, names of potential candidates for each of these schools, taking into consideration the fact that the candidates must be sought among the best militants and *not among volunteers*; 2) It is necessary for the Section leaderships to choose from those comrades who have proved themselves during the electoral campaign and the protest actions and political battles during the last few months.' (Archives Marty, Carton F-G, Dossier 8. CRHMSS, Université de Paris, 9 rue Malher, Paris 75004.)
34. Interviews with Albert Coïc, 18 June 1991(Caen); Danièle Garnier, 25 November 1991 (Caen); Claude Poperen, 1 April 1992 (Paris); Michel Pouchin, 17 June 1991 (Caen); Yannick Rauyer, 20 February 1992 (Caen). See also Kriegel, *French Communists*, p.265.
35. See note 46.
36. Interview with Gérard Leneveu, 20 February1992. Thus, Leneveu disputed the use of the word 'promotion': 'I don't like that term! In the Party, there are no careerists!' Yet, he had to admit: 'However, every time that I attended a party school I was rewarded with higher responsibilities.'
37. M. Offerle, *Les partis politiques* (Paris, 1987), p.78.
38. D. Gaxie, 'Economie des parties et rétributions du militantisme', p.136.
39. Offerle, *Les partis politiques*, p.74; Gaxie, 'Economie des parties et rétributions du militantisme', p.151; Kriegel, *French Communists*, p.198.
40. Gaxie, 'Economie des partis et rétributions du militantisme', p.142. Antoine Spire (*Profession permanent*, Paris, 1980, p.244) gives a graphic description of his life after leaving the Party and losing his job at *Editions sociales*: 'I experienced total emptiness after total fullness. There was the anguish of a certain inactivity after the anguish of a certain activism. After having enjoyed the warmth of being within the communist family I now feared the cold outside this family. [...] Overnight, I found myself with nothing. I am frightened. There is talk about unemployment. My wife and children have suffered excessively because of this break-up. I am still unable to tell my eldest son Nicolas—who asked me to complete a school questionnaire—what to write in the space 'father's profession..'.
41. Maurice Duverger, *Political Parties: their organization and activity in the modern state*. (London, 1978 edn), p.155.
42. Interview with Etienne Fajon 13 September 1991, Fajon, *Ma vie s'appelle liberté* (Paris, 1976), p.98.
43. Interview with Marie-Claire Lavabre, 13 September 1991.
44. Marie-Claire Lavabre, 'Etude d'une population de cadres communistes : le comité fédéral de Paris', *Communisme* 2, 1977, p.35. Jean Elleinstein, *Le P.C.* (Paris, 1976), p.183.
45. Offerle, *Les partis politiques*, pp.48–9.

46. Gaxie, 'Economie des partis et rétributions du militantisme', pp.131, 134–5.
47. Kriegel, *The French Communists*, p.188. Kriegel explains that the figure of 100,000 cadres is an arbitrary one. It is the result of an addition in which the same militants are counted twice (or even more often) because they have different functions at different levels. Nevertheless, as Kriegel puts it, 'it does give an idea of the size'.
48. M. Offerle, *Sociologie des groupes d'intérêt* (Montchrestien, Paris, 1998 edn), p.97.
49. Gaxie, 'Economie des partis et rétributions du militantisme', p.130.
50. Thus the study of Marxism-Leninism was always paralleled by the study of party history, the incarnation of Marxism-Leninism.
51. Meyer, *Moulding*, p.126.

The *Mot Dag* Association
'Leftist academics preaching radical ideas'
Geir Bentzen

Mot Dag was the name of both a journal and of an association of young Norwegian academics from 1921 to 1936. The name means 'Towards Day'. The members of *Mot Dag*, the '*motdagistene*', came to hold high positions in the Norwegian Civil Service and society in general. In the 1950s, at the peak of Labour Party hegemony, many of the old *Mot Dag* members held leading positions, and continued to do so well into the 1960s, and even into the 1970s in some cases. This means that *Mot Dag* is still remembered in Norway. Often even young people recognise the name and associate it with student radicalism. The natural way of introducing civil servants, politicians and others, was often not only to present their present titles and occupations; they were presented as former *motdagists* as well. *Mot Dag* as a political reality is not so well known today, but the myth and the magic are still there. It was the glue that bound the clerks of the strong state together.

Mot Dag is of interest for a number of reasons. It represented a cohort of young intellectuals drawn from Norway's old administrative upper class, perhaps radicalised by the impact of the First World War and Bolshevik revolution, but possibly too seeing in links with the ascendant labour movement the possibility of securing its own position against a 'new' upper class based on money. On the other hand, a reductionist view of this process is belied by the particularly fluid relationship it reveals between these leftist intellectuals, the Norwegian Labour Party, perceptions of the new Soviet Russia and the Communist International. Not only was *Mot Dag* a collective affiliate of the Norwegian Labour Party from March 1922 until its expulsion for indiscipline in August 1924, but the Labour Party itself was at that time and until the end of 1923 a section of the Comintern. As these anomalies were resolved, *Mot Dag* to some extent was continuously torn between the two. At the Comintern's Fourth Congress in 1922, it was decided, against the protests of the Norwegian delegates, that as a closed association it should be dissolved, and its journal transformed into a party organ. However, the association's leader, Erling Falk, was in this critical period an ally of the strong man in the Labour Party, Martin Tranmael, who was determined to limit the Comintern's influence with in the party. In February 1923 Tranmael regained the upper hand within the party by the passing of the so-called Kristiania Proposal which sought to diminish Comintern influence in local questions and maintain the party's autonomy nationally[1] Bukharin himself was snubbed when he demanded that a choice be made between Falk, and through him Tranmael, and good relations with the Comintern. Further controversy ensued that June when at the extended Comintern executive in Moscow Falk was criticised for an allegedly antisemitic article in *Mot Dag* attacking Radek. Zinoviev even claimed that *Mot Dag* was a fascist organisation.[2] Nevertheless, in November 1923 the party congress again gave majority support to Tranmael and Falk, with the result that the Norwegian Labour Party was immediately excluded from the Comintern and the defeated minority left to form the Communist Party of Norway (NKP). Ironically, Falk and Tranmael had by this time fallen out over a battle for the editorship of the party's daily newspaper, and henceforth *Mot Dag* was to lose its central position in the party.

Nevertheless, it survived another thirteen years. For two years, from December 1926, it was an affiliate of the Communist Party, and thereafter remained a declared communist group without formal ties to any party. It continued its work among students and intellectuals until in 1936 it was dissolved and its members, minus erstwhile leader Falk, assimilated into the governing Labour Party. However, it is on the earlier critical period that I wish to concentrate in this article, with special emphasis on the *motdagists'* understanding of the new Russia. While *Mot Dag* always followed the development of the Soviet Union with great interest, it never allowed itself to become dependent upon it, and as we have seen both collaborated with the Comintern, and through it the Soviet Union, and came into conflict with it. I therefore give special attention to the perceptions of Soviet Russia expressed in the pages of the journal in 1921–2, and the later impressions of key motdagist Trond Hegna—second only in prominence to Falk himself—after a visit there in 1929. From a distinctly Norwegian perspective, *Mot Dag* may be seen to provide new insights into the international phenomenon of the 'fellow-traveller', and relations between Soviet socialism and western traditions of progressive social reform.

The shaping of the new

The *Mot Dag* association sprang from talk and discussion activities in the Social Democratic Student Union in Kristiania (Oslo). Both here and in mainstream student society, the Russian revolution and the settlement after the First World War were focal issues during the first years of peace.[3] Trygve Bull and Trond Hegna both point out that the way the Western powers treated Germany was a crucial factor in the intense political life of student society from 1918 onward.[4] Both near and far parts of the world were politically unstable. The old system broke down on all fronts, and the key question was the shaping of the new.[5]

In the spring of 1920, Erling Falk participated in a study circle about capitalism led by professor Edvard Bull, and he followed the meetings of the Social Democratic Student Union. This must have been one of the few places where Erling Falk hardly spoke. Instead, according to Hegna, he invited younger students he had noticed at the meetings to restaurants.[6] There, the debate on the topics of the day continued.[7] Falk had lived several years in America, and was now building a business in Kristiania. He was both older than his new friends, and in a completely different economic situation from theirs. Again according to Hegna, one of them, Axel Sømme, addressed Falk at a meeting because he found it strange that such an eager listener never spoke himself. Falk then invited Sømme and some other friends to his apartment for further conversation. Sømme, Viggo Hansteen, John and Arnold Hazeland and a few others, Hegna writes, came to the apartment. This meeting is believed to be the start of the *Mot Dag* association.[8]

The participants came from the circle of students that Falk had got to know from 1919 onwards. They were all born in the period from 1896 to 1900, though Falk himself was born in 1887. All except two became students in 1918. *Mot Dag* can thus be considered a cohort, all students in 1918, and a generation, most of whom were born within the decade 1895–1905. In addition to those listed by Hegna as participating in the founding meeting, Trygve Bull mentions the following as the first members of the *Mot Dag* association: Hegna, Åke Anker Ording, Johan Vogt and Arne Ording. Others closely connected were apparently Hans Gabriel Dedichen, Hans Bogen and Ernst Suhrke, better known by the name Sigvang. True to the fashion of the time, the Social Democratic Student Association changed its name in 1920 to the Students' Communist Association and decided to issue a journal. Erling Falk became the key person in this work, and Viggo Hansteen's mother suggested the name '*Mot Dag*'. This name belongs to a European class of names. In Amsterdam, contemporary young radical architects named their social complex of flats *De Daagerad*, or 'dawn' in English. Other names from this class could be *Clarté—Claridad*, *Vorwärts* and the Norwegian journal *Veien frem* in the 1930s. They all carry connotations of the future and of enlightenment.

Falk created an editorial board for the journal consisting of students with whom he had developed a close contact. The cohort and the generation were thus knit together under the influence, control and power of one man. All others were excluded and even Trygve Bull conceded this tendency to exclusiveness in the society.[9] Later there would appear a number of rules that served to strengthen the elite character of the society. Participation meant activity and discipline. Members had an obligation to work for the society through a number of theme groups, but only two months after the formal foundation of the society, it was necessary to remind members that the obligation to work meant, as a minimum, that they turned up to the fortnightly meetings.[10] Consecutive non-appearances would mean being struck from the member list. The members also had to give all of their income to the society. In general *Mot Dag* was a disciplined fellowship of work for those members who chose to be really active. What that meant was best seen during the long summer of 1933, when the *motdagists* assembled at a rented farm to speed up their work with the *Workers' Encyclopaedia*. The discipline was so strict that Wilhelm Evang, later chief of the Norwegian Intelligence Agency, was sent to bring back two young men aged 25 and 28 who had sneaked away to meet local girls at a dance.[11]

Trond Hegna was of the opinion that for Falk a number of fundamental ideas lay behind the creation of *Mot Dag*. One of them was that world capitalism could disintegrate at any time. The working class had to be ready to take power when that occurred. That is why Falk went very strongly for an organisational system and the goals that seemed to follow as a consequence of 'the short revolutionary perspective', Hegna said. From this followed the concentration on an elite of highly qualified and active academics. Whether Falk realised this, or whether he had studied Lenin, is a question Hegna left open. The group from the Students' Communist Society that followed Falk was in any case less consistent in its loyalty to the Comintern, than was another early group led by Ole Colbjørnsen. After a short period Falk's group won the fight over members, and Colbjørnsen himself joined *Mot Dag*.

What started as a group of students within a student association rapidly developed into the editors of a journal, and from that into a student society in itself with its own journal. The journal was the most important public part of the society's work, and it probably gives the most correct picture of what they stood for. The articles were often signed by an author, but in reality they were written within the framework of the collective. They were debated and changed before the final version was printed. The result must be seen as the collective opinion of *Mot Dag*, not the opinion of a single author.

The first issue was published on 10 September 1921. It carried the subtitle 'Academic journal'. Axel Sømme was editor, within a short time to be replaced by the Sigurd Hoel, an author well-known in Norway. Hoel was told that he would be given ample help with the editing work from the society, something he later called a gross mis-statement.[12]

The journal was aimed at the intellectual reader, not based on formal qualifications alone, but on unbiased thinking.[13] It was to be a young journal for those who believed in themselves and in the future. There would be no place for 'the barren and blasé scepticism that characterises a decaying culture'. As with so many others, the ties were knit with the First World War. The publishers had 'matured' under the impression of the war and less than three years later the impression was still clear. The article that set out their programme contained a number of elements that would be repeated over and over again by a number of people who saw hope in Soviet Communism. These were elements like mass death, cultural destruction and the treason of the clerks or intellectuals, as Julien Benda later called it. The *motdagists* knew they belonged to a privileged elite, but they saw no need for the self-proletarianisation of the 1968 generation. On the contrary, they intended to develop their faculties and build a new society together with the workers.

A common point of view about who exactly the *motdagists* were is presented in Bull's 1955 biography about the association and its dominant figure, Falk:

> Young, resourceful men that due to misunderstood idealism wasted their youth to follow a dreamer and adventurer on a long trek through the desert. When they finally came to realise the truth, it was the more thorough, and they accordingly made successful careers fast. Today, these people are instrumental in governing the Norwegian welfare state.[14]

Bull himself did not agree with this characterisation. His opinion was that as academics, they had a specific role to fulfil in Norwegian democracy. In the *Mot Dag* period, university students were mostly recruited from a limited social group. Students from influential families with a Danish or German background still dominated. Bull believed it was of great importance that students from the higher social classes supported the politically radical side. This was not something new in Norway. In the previous century, politicians with bourgeois backgrounds had to a relatively large degree shown a radical disposition.[15] The Soviet Representation in Oslo had earlier pointed this out to its own authorities in the Soviet Union.[16] For Bull, the egalitarian ethics of Christianity, combined with radicalism and industrial capitalism, created the basis for producing academics with an ideological and radical attitude to form the socialist labour movement. However, Bull is not always an ideal source: he was too young to be present as Falk gathered his circle, shaping the *Mot Dag* association, and would never grow to be as central in the association as the men from the initial circle. On top of that, he married Falk's niece. Trond Hegna, who also discussed *Mot Dag* in his memoirs, was an earlier and more central player, and though politically never completely aligned with Falk, they were personally close for many years. Falk was of the opinion that Hegna was more of a Hegelian.[17]

First Secretary Semjon Mirny at the Representation in Oslo saw *Mot Dag* as

> an extremely leftist intellectual bourgeois grouping, whose members can only mistakenly be considered communists. The motdagist organization is a group of typical leftist academics preaching radical ideas. Through their social background they are representatives of the bourgeoise and academic circles who in their youth go through a radical period. Such is the tradition in the Norwegian academic public ever since the political battle over the national-political disbandment of the union with Sweden. This tradition lives on in these leftist organizations where not a single worker is member.[18]

Mirny did not recommend co-operation in 1931.

But Mirny did not understand that, even in Norway, the old times were gone. Rather than reverting to their basic conservative stand in defending the establishment, the *motdagist* group kept enough of their revolutionary attitude to enter into an alliance with the reformists, and actually became reformists themselves. Bull was of the opinion that the *motdagists* represent an upper class that felt declassed.[19] This opinion did not originally come from Bull and was presented by Arne Ording as early as 1921.[20] Ording felt that the cultural powers of resistance of the upper class were weakened, but at the same time said that the 'former upper class, the civil servant class' were the carriers of a culture that 'to a certain extent was of some value'. The new upper class was, in other words, built on money, the former upper class was to a certain extent built on culture. The *motdagist* individuals basically originated from this old upper class. To take this perspective a bit further, it is not the ideology and the good intentions that are the most prominent characteristics. Rather, one can see a generation of young men responding to the change of role given or forced upon them by the expanding business society, by associating with the mass movement shown through the Russian revolution to have the capacity to take power. It may seem that this generation makes an attempt to reconquer control by taking on the role of clerks to the labour movement, thereby defining the terms and conditions for the practical shaping of labour movement politics as it had to be applied at a takeover of power.

If we follow the careers of the *motdagist* individuals, such a perspective actually fits to a certain degree. Rather than the Norwegian labour movement having to develop its own intellectuals, as Gramsci considered necessary, it could take over a ready-made solution consisting of the sons of the old regime. But if this were really the case, it would be of the greatest importance to the *motdagist* group to be part of the strongest wing of the local labour movement, and not of a losing wing or of parts of the movement wanting to reduce the influence of the clerk regime for the benefit of others. But hardly anyone, and certainly no significant number of the *motdagists*, thought in this way about their participation in *Mot Dag*. What we see is the form of behaviour that we usually refer to as 'fashion'.

The upper class background of the *motdagists* gave them a special insight into the cultural decay of the new financial upper class, the nouveaux riches that rose during the war boom. For decades, Grand Kafé in Oslo had been the meeting place for academics and artists. Henrik Ibsen had his daily drink there. During the boom of the First World War, the cafe and other public areas of the hotel became the real stock exchange. Here one could find 18-year-olds drinking champagne or *pjolter*, highballs of whisky and soda water, buying shipping shares on credit, thereby gaining enormous wealth, or making them suffer just as enormous losses. The day when the government finally commanded an immediate 10 per cent downpayment at the purchase of shares, not a single well-known face was to be found at the cafe, only 'jobbers' trying to sell stock options. The pjolterjobbers squeezed the *motdagists*' class out.[21] It is not improbable that the *motdagists* despised the characters and social environment from the boom period. Given time, they would themselves drink their whisky without soda water.

Russia 1921–22

It is interesting to consider in this perspective the views expressed within the pages of *Mot Dag* about Soviet Russia. According to Viggo Hansteen, writing in September 1921, the hunger and the drought then devastating Russia had no connection with the ability of the Soviet government. On the contrary, it was by coincidence that the government had ended up with these constantly recurring phenomena to deal with. The consequences of the drought were made worse by the tsarist policies of the past, and it was to these that the present disastrous situation should still be attributed.[22] The reason why Russia had been able to export great amounts of grain before the war was that the population was systematically undernourished with three-fifths of the land in the hands of the state and the great landowners. The owners never invested in the necessary equipment to achieve decent productivity in the agriculture. They were not equipped to handle the difficult climatic conditions. Hansteen went on to criticise that the capital investments of the past few decades had not been made in agriculture but in industry, mining and the production of textiles for export. It would have been better for the economy if the investments had been concentrated in agriculture where four out of five had their living. Hansteen foresaw a slow economic growth, driven forward by a significant improvement in the productivity of agriculture through the use of capital goods. The industry he mentioned seems to consist of production to cover the needs of agriculture. As a final blow to any hope for fast improvement, he claimed that the Soviet Union had started a process that had taken 400 years in the West.

Hansteen saw only the needs of the moment, not the perspective of modernisation as a decisive factor for an improvement in the standard of living. A law student, Hansteen showed no knowledge about the ability of a modern industrial society to generate more wealth than a static, even modernised, agricultural society. He seemed not to think that the Soviet Union would need to catch up with the Western powers within a short time. In that he was not alone in 1921, but it seems significant that neither he, nor probably anybody else in *Mot Dag*, understood the basic connection between economic strength and the ability to create a better society for the people.

The most famous article in the journal in 1921 was Arne Ording's 'Why I am a communist'.[23] Just as François Furet would describe it by the end of the century, and as Henri Barbusse was to express it in *Clarté* just a few weeks later, Ording described a climate of debate where everything was connected with the war.[24] Primarily, Ording thought that the last years of the war and the peace treaties were decisive for his generation. This is logical. In these years the *motdagists* became adults and started to follow the war and its politics through the newspapers. It does not seem that the horrors of war made less of an impression in Norway than they did in France. That is by itself a characteristic of the internationalisation and modernisation of society. The near and the far away became of almost equal importance, and the war and the peace of Versailles were of importance even for Norwegian students. Class thinking took root; it became obvious that miners in Flanders and in Saxony had more in common with each other than they had with their masters. Forcing them to kill each other did not become less of a crime by that. At home, Ording's generation, and he used the word generation, had seen the effects of the boom times with the stockjobbers. Ording claimed that 'elements of lesser value in the people rose high and lived well off the squalor of war'. This argument lived on until a new war broke out in 1939, and was a forceful point of view in Nordahl Grieg's play *Our honour and our power*, from 1935.

All the wrongs of Norwegian society were made clearer: ' the unfairness was just as meaningless and distateful here as in the great powers of the world'. The young students could no longer stay out of politics, and they could not live in selfish isolation from society. Their feeling of social responsibility was awakened. They had to find a new way out of the disastrous situation, and that could only be a radical way. The treatment of Germany and the German people only strengthened the feeling that the world was off its tracks and that hypocrisy ruled. Ording then recited a poem by Arnulf Øverland:

> What is right has won
> A people is starved and slaughtered
> Now we have peace

Above all, Ording discussed how the First World War had shed a clear light on communist ideas. But his basic point of view was already more than sufficiently set out in his first few lines, and his readers could be in no doubt as to where he wanted to take them. The war was reason enough, and in 1921 there was one country and one country alone where the capitalism that had given rise to the war had been abandoned. Russia was betting its future on communism, and Ording and his fellows had found an economic and philosophical basis for the new society in communism.

As the Russian revolution passed its fourth anniversary, *Mot Dag* felt the need to comment upon the fact that the world press was far more positive towards Russia than earlier. That, it claimed, was because they now discerned a new sort of capitalism in the NEP policy, which they thought would destroy the proletarian dictatorship.[25] Many communists feared this policy. *Mot Dag* did not intend to make any excuses for the NEP policy, but rather to explain it, for it believed that what the communists in Russia did was to follow the movements within the Russian people. This populism was considered wise and likely to strengthen communist power, not weaken it.

And the world press had no reason for joy about western capitalism's survival. The Russian communists were the core troops of the Third International, *Mot Dag* reasoned, and they were working systematically to force the revolutionary breakthrough in the West. The Russian 'intelligence', defined mainly as university teachers, authors and students, had already in the nineteenth century been much more influenced by socialist ideas than their contemporaries in the West, according to Ording.[26]

A decisive influence

The *Mot Dag* society was thoroughly dominated by Erling Falk. These early years were the best years of his life. As age, cigarettes and whisky took their toll he was never to be the same again.[27] His influence over the development of the young men in *Mot Dag* was decisive. *Mot Dag* was a male fraternity for many years, and keeping it so was justified by the difficulties that responsibilities for wife and family would create for professional revolutionaries. Female members would lead to jealousy and involvement. Even women's female characteristics were criticised.[28] Trond Hegna began his close association with Falk when he felt that some members did not respect the restrictions concerning women, and sought out Falk to inform him that he intended to leave *Mot Dag* because of such unfaithfulness to the cause. Instead of accepting the resignation Falk offered to join Hegna in founding a new society. They both decided to stay on, but after the incident Hegna became clearly second only to Falk in the association. That meant being exposed to long nightly conversations, or rather, speeches from Falk, whose way of describing how leaders had been educated and trained in the past suggested that he felt they should remain single, and that the training ought to encompass being the confidante of the ruling leader.

A reader of the articles, speeches, memoirs and protocols of *Mot Dag*, cannot overlook the basic arrogance that lies behind them. The manner of their composition, the expressions and the points of view are entirely self-assured. Hegna later pointed to the effect a glass of whisky had on young men before or during the writing, but there is more to it than that.[29] What one observes is the security of the priviliged, for the social background and level of education of the *motdagists* made them almost untouchable. With time the state and society would employ them in influential and well-paid positions, just as had been the case with their fathers and grandfathers. In the meantime they lived off the family fortune or on money from their parents. To achieve things, one needs the security to be able to risk a loss. Losing must have forseeable and knowable consequences that can be neutralised later.[30] The *motdagists* probably felt that they were in precisely such a position.

There may be some doubt as to whether there is a clear connection between the members' original perceptions of Soviet Russia and the articles whch appeared in the first issues of the journal. Most of them had discussed the new Russia in meetings for more than three years before the first publication of the journal. Nevertheless, the journal is the best and earliest source we have. The 1921 and 1922 issues also benefit from being less preoccupied with internal Norwegian squabbling over the Soviet Union than would be the case later. Even by 1922, the introduction of a number of these internal elements of debate makes it difficult to assess whether the writers were discussing the Soviet Union per se, or a number of Norwegian party questions and traditions at the same time. But if in many ways major Norwegian policy questions became more dominant than international politics, it was always with the Third International looming in the background.

An article by Aake Anker Ording (Arne Ording's cousin) entitled 'Marx and the future' opened up the ideological horizons of the journal.[31] Marxism as a science, he wrote, had to play a secondary role to both the truth and to clear logic. The communist workers' party had to be based on healthy feelings and strong instincts, not on love of dogmas. Those of its adversaries who claimed that communism was a sort of religion were right. The dream of a better society led to a willingness to give one's all in life for the cause, and that was not only a source of strength but of weakness for it carried with it a danger of mysticism and belief in dogmas. For too long, Ording went on, marxist materialism had been allowed to function as a dogma that answered all problems. Human psychology had to be brought into the picture too, and not just theories of economy:

> The values of society are not only based upon the land and the sum of productive forces and working hands, but maybe just as much on the will to work and the happiness of work.

A former reformist chairman of the Labour Party, the wealthy lawyer Ludvig Meyer, was quoted as to the importance of feelings. The entire social problem and its solutions had to be found within the framework of work and motivation.

One may well believe that it was not just Ludvig Meyer that had influenced Ording. Falk himself had a well-known admiration for everything American and for Henry Ford in particular. Ording argued for an ideology that not only was based upon Marxism and Leninism, but also on the strongest argument of capitalism, that is, the personal drive to create something. In January 1922 that seemed in line with the NEP policy in the Soviet Union, though that in itself was a policy that strayed from Marxist-Leninism. Ording may be regarded as having integrated the NEP policy into the basic ideology of the *motdagists*. Viewed alongside his warnings about the power or perhaps the theology of dogmas and the 21 points of the Comintern, the contours of a decisive split between the *motdagist* communism and that of the Comintern become visible.

Ording's arguments were strengthened by Falk himself. He reiterated that *Mot Dag* worked for a communist society as a workers' state.[32] But the living conditions of the workers were so dismal that they had to be improved here and now. That did not mean that bourgeois society was to be saved from decay, but under prevailing conditions one could not expect the workers to join a revolutionary fight for a communist revolution. It was therefore correct not to let oneself be tied to distant and debatable programmes. All forces had to be concentrated on comprehensible short-term improvements, and that meant a certain understanding for the employers' demands for a reduction of salaries in order to avoid mass unemployment. In turn, guarantees not to reduce the present level had to be given by the employers, so that reductions in salaries did not only amount to a postponement of mass unemployment. A way to revolution might be to demand that the salaries be set at a fixed value and in future rise in parallel with the loss of value of the Norwegian Krone, according to an index decided by the Labour Party itself. Within a few months, this scheme would break the bourgeois economy, bourgeois society would have to relinquish its obligations, the revolution could be identified with the fight for a decent salary, and *Mot Dag* and the Labour Party could show that they did not only seek revolution as an 'artificial and impractical solution'. On the contrary, it would appear a necessity for the workers to keep their standard of living, and it would mould the whole working class together in a strong revolutionary show of will.

The new Russia, 1929–30

Trond Hegna's views after his visit to the USSR in 1929 provide an interesting point of comparison with contributions on the same subject a few years earlier. It is quite possible that Hegna's views, at the moment when collectivisation and the five-year plans were being initiated, were clearer and more militant than those which most *motdagists* would have formulated for themselves. All facts about Russia could not carry the same weight, Hegna wrote, and the perspective taken had to be of world historic proportions. He used both Bismarck the statesman and Abraham Lincoln as examples. They were evaluated not on the basis of the level of suffering their policies had created, but on the results they achieved. They were both able to stomach the sufferings.[33] Hegna, contrary to Falk, was considered a Hegelian.[34] Only the totality carried significant meaning. Singular facts were of importance only as parts of the totality. Where Hegel praised the Prussian state as an expression of general will in its highest form, Hegna accorded the Soviet Union the same position, with Stalin performing the world-historical role that Napoleon had played in Hegel's time.[35]

The internal power struggles in the Russian party were seen as parts of a Hegelian totality. Hegna thought that Stalin's destiny would be the same as that of his opponents, when his time was up:

> As long as Stalin incarnates the overview, the will and the action in the present development in Russia, he will continue to occupy the unique position of leadership he now has. The day he no longer dominates the development will be the day he is thrown aside. There will, however, almost certainly not be one of the other old and known leaders who will take his place. There are thousands upon thousands of of young bolsheviks created by the revolution ready to fill any vacant position the revolution will place them in.

Russia's way would make it a great power of a new type, that is one of the two remaining great powers by 1940, the Soviet Union and the United States of America. Great Britain and Japan would both have to attach themselves to one of these. This perspective did not originate from Hegna—he was paraphrasing the New York Times—but there is no doubt that he agreed with it. The revolution would never have happened if Russia had lacked an elite to lead the masses. The workers and the peasants would surely have risen against their masters, but they would have lacked a clear view of what to do and how a new society should look.[36] The necessary elite was organised in the Communist Party under the leadership of Lenin and now Stalin. Their basic philosophy was Marxism.

Hegna then went on to explain Russian Marxism, but did not mention the philosophical currents that shaped the Russian Marxism Lenin created.[37] The Marxism of Hegna was modernistic, built on an admiration for the creativity of the bourgeoisie and its achievements in technology and science. This was following good *motdagist* tradition by mixing the most attractive elements of revolutionary Marxism and the creativity and productivity of Western free enterprise. Erling Falk himself did this repeatedly.

Free enterprise itself suffered from the effects of the economic crisis capitalist society had created. The development of production and machinery was hindered by the crisis. It was clear that further development within science and technology demanded a new form of society. That had to be the society of the workers because the working class was the only class of society that had been created by modern society. The working class was not bound to older forms of society like all other classes. Its principles of organisation were far more advanced than the principles followed by the rest of society. Proletarian dictatorship did not mean that all had to be proletarian, a thought abhorred by the *motdagists*; it meant that the organisational principle of the working class was made the principle of society. By following the principle, Russia had been able to rebuild after the civil war. From 1921 to 1926 things were achieved that western experts had deemed would take decades and demand the import of capital.

The impressions and thoughts Trond Hegna accumulated on his journey to Russia in 1929 make up the basic background for his book of 1931. Where Viggo Hansteen's was a static account in 1921, Hegna's was dynamic. He praised the technological development and the new five-year plan, and had no doubts about the plans to double the industrial output in general, and to triple the output of industrial machinery. For Hegna, collectivisation and five-year plans were part of the necessary dynamic of modernisation.

His belief in the system was total. He allowed no doubts and no insecurity to penetrate his writings about Soviet society and its future. No better and no more modern society existed. Above all it probably was a historically correct society for Hegna and a test case of future society. The totality of his commitment was strengthened by the many formidable facts he presented: the democratic elections with an almost 100 per cent participation, a constitution built on the needs of working life, competition among the different units within an industry, and not least the important participation in politics of experienced managers from industry. Hegna's political perspective was mainly concentrated on production, as suited a society whose norms were given in masses and volume. Parallel to his denial of the existence of slave work in the Soviet Union, he did admit that the Russians lived a strict life. It was puritan and spartan to build the future.[38] A few years later the Norwegian author Nordahl Grieg found pleasure in the same observation.

The New Russia had a special position in the world of *Mot Dag*. All hope for the future was tied up with its development. Though Hegna came close in 1931, the Soviet Union was never considered a realised utopia, only a utopia under construction. More important than the results hitherto achieved was the process adopted to achieve them. The methods of the regime had to be evaluated in a world historical perspective, and that meant that they were of less importance than the goals which were set out. That may turn out to have been the enduring link between these Soviet enthusiasms and the welfare society established by Labour governments in Norway. Their period in *Mot Dag* taught a generation of Norwegian academics to create ideologically defined quantitative goals for the development of society, and it taught them how to participate in and win a debate for the subsequent exercise of power. Even though they lost their belief in the Soviet Union later in life, they never lost the conviction that much could be learned from the experiment.

Notes

1. Kristiania, earlier Christiania, was the name of Oslo from 1624 to 1925.
2. 'Radek og andre' (Radek and others), *Mot Dag*, no. 4 (1923), pp.25–27. Not signed, but known to be written by Haakon Meyer.
3. Trygve Bull, *Mot Dag* og Erling Falk (Oslo, 1955), pp.7–37.
4. Trond Hegna, *Min versjon* (Oslo, 1983), pp.30–5.
5. The German question and the Versailles Treaty kept their significance: Ludvig Meyer, 'Religion og dans', *Mot Dag*, 14 January 1922.
6. Hegna, Min versjon, pp.41–2.
7. Erling Falk's background was closely followed by Bull, *Mot Dag*.
8. Hegna, *Min versjon*, pp.42–3.
9. Bull, *Mot Dag*, p.31–2, 35.
10. Protocol of meetings 1922–1923, meeting 20 May 1922, *Mot Dag* archive Aa-001, Archive and Library of the Labour Movement (AAB), Oslo.
11. Bull, *Mot Dag*, p.266.
12. Hegna, *Min versjon*, pp.501, 53, 578, 56.
13. Programmatic article, *Mot Dag*, 10 September 1921.
14. Bull, *Mot Dag*, p.288.
15. Bull, *Mot Dag*, pp.56–65, 289.
16. File 495–99–33, pp.61–3, The Russian State Archive for Social and Political History (hereafter RGASPI), Moscow; File 5283–1a–172, The Federal Russian State Archive (hereafter GARF), Moscow.
17. Bull, *Mot Dag*, pp.290, 117.
18. File 495–99–33, pp.61–3, RGASPI; File 5283–1a–172, GARF.
19. Bull, *Mot Dag*, p.84.
20. Arne Ording, 'Tale ved det akademiske massemøte mandag 5 September 1921' , *Mot Dag*, 24 September 1921.
21. Mentz Schulerud, *På Grand i hundre år*, 1874–1974 (Oslo, 1974), pp.178–83.
22. Viggo Hansteen, 'Hvorfor sulter Rusland?' *Mot Dag*, 10 September 1921.
23. Arne Ording, 'Tale ved det akademiske massemøte, mandag 5 September 1921', *Mot Dag*, 24 September 1921.
24. François Furet, *Den tapte illusjon—Et essay om den kommunistiske idé i det 20. århundre* (Oslo, 1996), pp.52–86; Clarté, no. 1, 19 November 1921.
25. 'Fra Fronten', *Mot Dag*, 19 November 1921. Not signed.
26. Arne Ording, 'Intelligensens tragedie i Rusland', *Mot Dag*, 31 December 1921.
27. Hegna, *Min versjon*, pp.61–3.
28. Hegna, *Min versjon*, pp.64–69; Hegna pointed to 'En fortælling uten moral', *Mot Dag*, 2 September 1922, a poem by A.M. Clifford. He believed Falk and Hansteen were behind the pseudonym Clifford.
29. Hegna, *Min versjon*, pp.70–1, 57.
30. Geir Bentzen, *En vurdering av kulturens betydning i norske bedrifter med henblikk på ledelsesform og videreutvikling*, Thesis for the Diploma of Oslo School of Business Administration, Oslo, 1984.

31. Aake Anker Ording, 'Marx og fremtiden', *Mot Dag*, 14 January 1922.
32. Erling Falk, 'Foran vaarkampen', *Mot Dag*, 11 February 1922.
33. Trond Hegna, *Det nye Russland* (Fram, Oslo, 1931), pp.3–4.
34. Bull, *Mot Dag*, p.117.
35. Trond Hegna, *Sovjet, Stalin og generalene* (Oslo, 1937), p.35; Hegna, *Russland*, p.25.
36. Hegna, *Russland*, pp.5–6.
37. Tibor Szamuely, *The Russian Tradition* (London, 1988).
38. Hegna, *Russland*, pp.7–8, 10–11, 13, 20–23, 15–17, 19.

Reviews

Books to be remembered (4)

Jessica Mitford, *The Making of a Muckraker*, New York, 1975; London, 1979

This is one of the lesser known books of Jessica Mitford, at least in this country. She belonged to an extraordinary family. Her father was Lord Redesdale and the tumultuous life of the family of five sisters and one brother are described in the first volume of her autobiography *Hons and Rebels*. Of her sisters, Nancy was the well-known novelist; Deborah became the Duchess of Devonshire; Diana married Sir Oswald Mosley; and Unity was a devoted admirer, and friend, of Adolf Hitler. Jessica from her early days was and remained a political radical, and for a number of years was a member of the American Communist Party, the object of several bouts of inquisition from the un-American activities groups.

In her early days she broke with the family and went to Republican Spain with her cousin Esmond Romilly, who was also a nephew of Winston Churchill. Esmond joined a fighting unit for several months and on their return to England they married, and at the beginning of the Second World War they were in the United States. Esmond volunteered for active service, joined the Canadian RAF and was killed in 1943.

Jessica remained in California and later married Bob Treuhaft, a well-known and very active civil rights lawyer. He was counsel to the dockers on the East Coast, and it was his growing concern with the high costs of funerals among his clients that encouraged Jessica to begin her investigations into the death industry. Her results were staggering, and the book that described the quite extraordinary costs that were being charged by the funeral businesses became a nationally read text. *The American Way of Death*, published in 1963, was a revelation. It provided many examples of ways in which the morticians charged as high as possible costs for funeral expenses. The stories are often gruesome and the whole analysis was backed by a stream of personal interviews with funeral directors from all over the United States. There was a meeting with a funeral director who explained why he always recommended a pure silk lining for the casket lining although it was more expensive than rayon: 'We find rayon is a lot more irritating to the skin'.

The Making of a Muckraker is a collection of essays and articles, mostly written after the 1963 book. Most are accounts of her further investigations into various corrupt, unethical practices as well as additional stories of her most famous book. She wrote an article a year or so after publication in which she explained that largely because of her current failure to find publishers she expected little publicity. When therefore *The American Way of Death* appeared the reception it received was, in her words, 'so totally unexpected that I still have not recovered from the excitement of it all'. Sales were huge and newspapers and journals, TV and radio took up the criticisms of what Jessica usually referred to as the 'death industries'. It became a national topic of comment and conversation and Jessica was inundated with letters from all over the continent.

The reaction of the funeral business community was bitter, of course. They rounded on Jessica 'in absolute fury'. In their journals—*Casket and Sunnyside*; *Concept: The Journal of Creative Ideas for Cemeteries*—'the Mitford Bomb', 'the Mitford war-dance' and so on appeared regularly. Her radical politics were brought in to explain her generally subversive attitudes, and a Californian Congressman read a two-page statement about her subversive background into the Congressional Record. Her suggestions for funeral simplicity, thereby reducing sharply the total costs, were denounced as 'atheistic Communism'. As a leading national official explained: 'Funerals are becoming more and more a part of the American way of life'.

At the beginning of this book, Jessica provided an interesting and very useful statement of how she went about her investigations. Here is her introduction:

> In this collection I have tried to reconstruct my own efforts, over a twenty-year period, to acquire these qualities and to demonstrate, through one person's experience, the development of investigative techniques. In the comment accompanying each group or group of pieces, I have sought to convey something of the story-behind-the-story: how I stumbled into the particular subject; the joys and sorrows of research, the lucky breaks and mistakes, things overlooked through sheer ineptitude for which one could kick oneself; difficulties of getting published; and in some cases afterglow of satisfaction ... (and, she added, 'plodding determination and an appetite

for tracking and destroying the enemy'.)

There is no better illustration of Jessica's general approach than her chapter entitled 'My short and happy life as a Distinguished Professor'. It began in May 1973 when the acting chairman of the Department of Sociology at San Jose State University in California wrote to Jessica and asked whether she would be interested to be considered as a Distinguished Professor for a semester. She did not know at the time that the same letter had been sent to 25 other persons, but she was chosen and took up the post in September 1973 for four months. She was expected to provide sustenance for two classes: one, a major lecture weekly to about 200 students, and then a small honours group of about twenty.

Jessica had no academic credits of any kind. Lady Redesdale had not believed in girls going to school, so Jessica had never been to primary school, secondary school or university. She spent the summer before taking up her appointment in being guided through the usual academic procedures but more importantly, in bringing together the materials for her courses. She decided that the major course would be titled 'The American way', the final section of which would be 'Water-buggers of yesteryear'. This would include the witch-hunting of the left after 1945. The head of the San Francisco FBI would be invited to explain the procedures for electronic surveillance of suspected subversives, and there would be judges, lawyers and ex-convicts to talk on their interests. The small seminar would be concerned with 'The techniques of muckraking'.

Her unusual type of lecture was obviously going to provide much interest and no doubt critical comment from both inside and outside the university. Her appointment had already been met with considerable opposition from the highest level of administrators, but this was a situation which Jessica was happy to confront. What, however, she was not aware of at the beginning of her appointment were two requirements from all new members of the academic staff. These were signing the loyalty oath, and her fingerprinting. After a long discussion with sympathetic colleagues she signed the loyalty oath, but continued to refuse the fingerprint obligation. There was a major upheaval on the campus and the Department of Sociology backed her with much vigour; as did the students. There were matters taken to court and once again Jessica began to appear in the national press. While her case had made it legally correct to refuse fingerprinting, the university administration continued with the practice and Jessica naturally considered this her failure. She had a personal consolation. After the article on her experiences had been published in the *Atlantic* journal (October 1974), the Dean of Calhoun College, Yale, wrote inviting her to teach a seminar on

'Muckraking and investigative journalism'. He added that neither the loyalty oath nor fingerprinting were requirements for the position.

This is a book to be enjoyed, with full recognition to Jessica Mitford's courage (and pleasure) at her sorties against the ignorance and money grubbing of so many in the world around her. A great woman.

John Saville
Professor emeritus at the University of Hull and president of the
Oral History Society

Art is the tool of universal progress

Margarita Tupitsyn (ed.) *El Lissitzky: Beyond the Abstract Cabinet: Photography, design, collaboration* (Yale University Press, New Haven and London, 1999), ISBN 0 30008 170 7, 239pp., £40.00 hbk.

Lazar [Eliezer or Eleazar] Markovich Lissitzky (1890–1941) was born in the Smolensk region of Russia, growing up in Vitebsk and Smolensk. From 1909 to 1914 he studied architecture—and drawing at the Technical Institute of Darmstadt in Germany. At the outbreak of the Great War of 1914–18, Lissitzky returned to Russia, continuing his studies at the Riga Polytechnic Institute, then relocated to Moscow. After the October Revolution of 1917 Lissitzky worked in the Section of Visual Arts of the People's Commissariat of Enlightenment (*IZO Narkompros*). In 1919 he headed the Workshops of Graphic and Printing Arts and Architecture at the Artistic-Technical Institute (*Khudozhestvenno-Prakticheskii Institut*) at Vitebsk established by Marc Chagall. There he designed propaganda posters and other projects (some with Kazimir Malevich) in abstract style. Malevich was, with Piet Mondrian, an early pioneer of pure abstraction in art, founding the Suprematist movement.

In an essay written in 1920, Lissitzky proclaimed:

> The artist constructs a new symbol with his brush. This symbol is not a recognizable form of anything in the world—it is a symbol of the new world which is being built upon and which exists by way of the people.

Lissitzky carried Suprematism beyond Malevich's original formulation of pure painting imbued with a spiritual aura.

> With their multiple references to real and abstract space, the Prouns became a system through which Lissitzky not only ruminated upon formal properties of transparency, opacity colour, shaper and line but began to dwell upon the deployment of these forms into socialized space, placing

him into the path of the emergence of Constructivism, which, using a similarly reductive visual vocabulary sought to merge art and life through mass production and industry.

In spite of Lissitzky's affinities with Russian Constructivism up to 1922 his work remained idiosyncratic, privileging aesthetics above utility. For him, constructive art could be successful as art only if its aesthetic programme remained dominant to technological considerations. This sentiment he continued to assert in the ensuing years.

When Lissitzky arrived in Berlin at the end of 1921, he was intent on making contact with artists from abroad. Berlin was then one of the great cultural capitals of Europe, fertile soil for Expressionism and Dada, and for vanguard art in all its diversity. It was also a strategic centre for the promotion of Soviet politics and culture. By 1920 more than one hundred thousand Russians of various persuasions had settled there. Among them was the writer Ilia Ehrenburg, who was affiliated with the Scythians, a group of intellectuals who supported the Russian Revolution but opposed Bolshevism. Ehrenburg became one of Lissitzky's close comrades. Together they published the trilingual periodical *Veshch-Gegenstand-Object* (1922), intended as an international journal of contemporary culture. The inaugural issue included interviews with such artists as Fernand Lèger and Gino Severini, and articles by Thee van Doesberg, Le Corbusier, and Nikolai Punin. The editorial championed constructive art, 'whose mission is not…to embellish life but to organize it'.

In 1925 Lissitzky returned to Russia to practise architecture. Shortly after, he resumed work in graphic design and photography that henceforth paralleled his architectural designs. He achieved recognition as a designer for exhibitions at home and abroad, for Soviet films, and for propaganda journals such as *USSR in Construction*. For his experiment in photomontage, Lissitzky coined the neologism '*fotopis*' (photo writing or photo scribing), which he juxtaposed to the photogram.

Ten years after the retrospective exhibition held to mark the centenary of Lissitzky's birth, the Sprengel Museum Hannover combined with the Museu d'Art Contemporani de Barcelona and the Fondação de Serralves, Porto, to present another large exhibition of Lissitzky's photographs and designs as well as his collaborative projects. The sturdy, beautifully made, lavishly illustrated quarto volume now reviewed is the scholarly *Catalogue Raisonné* of that latter exhibition. It illustrates for the first time the breadth and complexity of Lissitzky's career beyond his better known abstract production. It exemplifies the second phase of Soviet avant-garde art no longer abstract, but now defined by the use of photography, photomontage and film.

The author of this ground breaking and fascinating study, Margarita Tupitsyn, an independent scholar and curator, includes extensive contributions by Matthew Drutt, associate curator for research at the Guggenheim Museum, and by Ulrich Pohlmann, director of the Foto Museum in Munich. Drutt explores the life and work of Lissitzky in Germany, 1922–5; Margarita Tupitsyn follows the artist back to Moscow; and Pohlmann focuses on Lissitzky's exhibition designs and, revealingly, on the significant influence of his work in Germany, Italy and the United States, 1923–43. Striking plates, many of them ingenious, dramatic, and vividly coloured, ennoble these pages. Here there are several experimental self-portraits of Lissitzky himself, along with photomontage portraits of avant-garde figures such as Hans Arp and Kurt Schwitters. Public and private collections worldwide are handsomely represented.

'Archive' assembles photos from Lissitzky's private archive and works by artists with whom he collaborated, such as Man Ray, Georgy Zimin, Sergei Senkinr Gustav Klutsisr Dziga Vertov, Ivan Shagin, Georgy Petrusov, Eduard Tisser, Solomon Telingater.

A collection of letters by Lissitzky, published in English for the first time by courtesy of the Getty Museum, is introduced and annotated by Margarita Tupitsyn. Two letters are to the German designer Jan Tschichold, the rest to Sophie Küppers, Lissitzky's wife of eight years, and increasingly his artistic collaborator, who moved to Moscow in 1927 from her native Germany. These letters provide a narrative that is repeatedly structured around three themes: his illness with tuberculosis, his and Küppers' relationship and personal life, and the circumstances of Lissitzky's work with mass media in general and on the photo album *Food Industry* in particular. The resulting entanglement of private and public affairs as they developed in the prewar period under Stalin explains why Lissitzky and his colleagues continued to serve the state regardless of the increasing pressure it placed upon their working techniques and artistic principles.

Tupitsyn is surely correct when she states:

> In Lissitzky's case his tuberculosis and his wife and three children forced him to rely on influential people whose power was the equivalent of medical insurance and could guarantee him a monthly income. Because the propaganda publications paid generously, many artists regarded them as a highly competitive source of income rather than simply as a mechanism of coercion or as an opportunity to display one's loyalty to a ruthless regime. (p.201)

This economic fact of life places Soviet image-makers surprisingly close to their Western counterparts!

> Lissitzky's letters demonstrate that no matter how much the design principles of the 1920s were degraded in the late examples of Soviet proaganda materials they should not be viewed as precursors of socialist realist methodology. Instead, they are concluding examples of agitational objects, as they had been envisioned since the Constructivists refuted painting in the early 1920s. (p.201)

The content of Lissitzky's letters, together with his career as outlined in this erudite volume, opens up new approaches to evaluating the history of the Soviet avant-garde. Tupitsyn concludes:

> No matter how ruptured that history is on the level of formal search, it is connected by the avant-gardists' continuous attempts to bridge art, politics and life. Along this path, the avant-garde practitioners were perpetually changing course, not only because of shifting political events but also because of the resistance of artists to accept a single mode of artistic production and distribution. With that aim the Soviet avant-garde disjointed itself not only from socialist realism, which defended static artistic strategies and depended on the status quo, but more important, from subsequent artistic manifestations of this century. (p.202)

A thorough chronology, from 1890 to 1941, a useful select bibliography (including works by El Lissitzky, Sophie Lissitzky-Küppers, and Jen Lissitzky), and a generally chronological catalogue of the exhibition, describing 274 items, round off this admirable, learned study, which complements two earlier, pioneering works by Margarita Tupitsyn; *Glaube, Hoffnung, Anpassung: Sowjetische Bilder, 1928–1945* (1995) and *The Soviet Photograph, 1924–1937* (1996). One can find here no sure answer to the always lingering question among Lissitzky scholars, as to what kind of artist would he have been had he not fallen ill with tuberculosis in 1923? Clear and indisputable from this superb, attractive study are the genius and imaginative intensity of Lissitzky's 'incomparable experiments', and their contemporary resonance.

H.G.A. Hughes

Miners and disaster

Stanley Williamson, *Gresford. The Anatomy of a Disaster* (Liverpool University Press, Liverpool, 1999) ISBN 0-85323-9, 243pp., £9.99 pbk.

Stanley Williamson has produced a long overdue account of one of the most devastating colliery disasters in the history of British mining. Not only does he provide an insight into the events leading up to the explosion at Gresford

Colliery in 1934 causing 266 deaths, but he also offers the historian the chance to explore the industrial relations of the neglected North Wales coalfield. The first chapter provides a dramatic account of the disaster seen through the eyes of miners who survived the tragedy. The reader is taken through the labyrinthine roadways and the perilous journey that survivors made to reach safety. Williamson provides an illuminating portrait of unscrupulous coal owners, brutal managers, and deferential workers.

Along with many other mines in the North Wales coalfield, Gresford does not fit easily with the popular image of the traditional mining community. Miners were drawn from a number of settlements in the greater Wrexham area, with many reluctant to move into the garden village that was constructed to attract labour. At the time of the disaster, Gresford was one of the biggest pits in the district employing 2,200 men and boys and was thus central to the district union in terms of membership and funds. However, before the disaster, the North Wales Miners Association (NWMA) only organised a third of employees.

The number of fatalities involved in the disaster was increased by the number of men who had opted to work the Friday night shift in order to attend the football match between Wrexham and Tranmere the following day. The incidence of overtime at the pit was a symptom of the company's desire to improve productivity and the inability of the miner to limit his hours due to the paucity of the wages paid by the company. The immediate aftermath of the disaster left the coalfield in a state of mourning compounded by widespread unemployment.

From painting a picture of the coalfield, the colliery, and the surrounding environment, the author moves on to a detailed account of the Court of Inquiry held in Wrexham, to ascertain what caused the explosion in the Dennis section of the pit. The NWMA from the outset felt that this calamity was not an 'act of God' and approached Stafford Cripps to represent them at the proceedings. The Miners Federation of Great Britain (MFGB) also sent leading figures such as Joseph Jones, Peter Lee and Joe Hall. Cripps put on a bravura performance in attacking the owners, the manager, and the colliery deputies. He claimed that they had all conspired to create an atmosphere of intimidation and negligence. In the course of the inquiry, Cripps was able to reveal the working environment of the colliery and the relationship between miners and management that led to a series of illegal actions in breaching safety regulations. The manager, William Bonsall, was the most recent in a line of Gresford managers who showed a disregard for safety. His attitude at the inquiry led to scenes of exasperation as he continually evaded questions. Bonsall was revealed to be a liar when Cripps proved that he had sanctioned the falsification of gas tests. The deputies also emerged as figures more concerned with productivity than their primary role as safety officials. The conflicting priorities of deputies was to be a source of much discontent throughout the rest of the century.

The main chapters dealing with inquiry form the body of the book and are its strongest sections. The outcome of the inquiry was inconclusive with each party providing their own reports. The NWMA and the MFGB remained convinced that continued breaches of safety measures led directly to the disaster. Representatives of the bereaved pressed for the reopening of the Dennis section of the pit for further investigation, but this was resisted by the inspectorate, with the scene of the explosion permanently sealed. Throughout the text, Williamson attempts to explain why Gresford contained a deferential workforce. The evidence he provides is rather sketchy and underdeveloped. Gresford was not alone in the coalfield in drawing men from a range of geographical locations and experiencing fluctuating levels of union membership. This was a feature of many pits in North Wales through to nationalisation. He then points to the attitude of the owners in thwarting attempts at unionisation. After the 1926 lockout, Gresford did not provide members of the breakaway union that had established itself at Point of Ayr, a move that would have surely been encouraged by the owners if they were so set against MFGB activity. The author then points to the 'buttysystem' of sub-contracting as being a contributory factor to the deferential attitude of the miners. The relationship between the 'butty-system' and moderation is too simplistic, as in other coalfields many 'butties' were union members themselves and the relationship between them and other miners was not always conflictual. The prevalence of the system was not only confined to moderate districts of the MFGB, as in the Kent coalfield 'butties' remained a prominent part of the workforce through to public ownership.

What appears in some of the oral testimonies, is the perception that the miners themselves held about the power of organised resistance to management initiatives. A Gresford miner stated at the inquiry that he did not take matters of safety up with the union, but he would have done at his previous pit in Yorkshire. This perception of the moderate nature of organised labour in the coalfield continued down the years, when miners arriving from Manchester in 1968 and Burnley in 1981 voiced criticism at the timidity of leaders in North Wales. The aftermath of the disaster signified a period of militancy in the coalfield. There was a violent strike at Bersham Colliery in 1935 and a campaign against the company union at Point of Ayr in Flintshire. All these events were presided over by a new leader of the district, Edward Jones, who Williamson wrongly claims was from Point of Ayr. Jones had in fact been a miner in the Wrexham district employed at Wynnstay and Llay. His hard work led to an almost fully unionised workforce in the coalfield by 1947. The success of Jones suggests that the situation at Gresford was as dependent on the strategy of the district leadership as it was on the intransigence of the owners.

Williamson has written a definitive source on the disaster that offers an insight into a neglected coalfield. The book also raises questions concerning the official inquiry that concealed more than it revealed in apportioning blame. The author has produced a welcome addition to the history of British miners, which should be of interest to both academics and the general reader.

Keith Gildart
Department of Politics, University of York

History for a new generation

Andrew Forrest, *The Spanish Civil War* (London, Routledge, 2000) ISBN 0 415 182115, x+150 pp., £6.99 pbk.

My generation lived through it. My own uncles, aunts and cousins were directly involved and sometimes it seems only yesterday that the Spanish War was front-page news. In fact it all happened sixty-five years ago, but here is Andrew Forrest making a brave effort to explain to 21st-century sixth-formers what it was all about. His book contains seven chapters, each with background material, and analysis, together with some sources, questions and even worked answers.

Although for any good history teacher such an undertaking is the core of his job, this subject raises formidable problems. Not only because across sixty-five years thousands of books and articles have poured unimaginable millions of words over those years 1936 to 1939, but because also you have to assess the standpoint and reliability of those who said they were there and saw it happen; you must judge the political axes that later interpreters ground so assiduously.

Forrest has tried to indicate the orientation of some of the witnesses he quotes, but this is not easy. Thus in Spain 'Marxist' did not necessarily mean 'Communist'; the Communist Party of Spain (PCE) was very small until 1936, and had only 16 of the 470 seats in the Cortes after the elections that February. The 'M' in the title of the anti-Moscow POUM stood for 'Marxist' and even some in the Socialist Party claimed themselves so. At the same time some 'Right Wing' groups were Catholic, others Monarchist, Catalan business groups and military organisations; while Basque Catholics were generally leftwing. Very little was clear cut in the Spain of the 1930s and the need to check thoroughly all evidence should be good training for students.

Again the Spanish War crystallised so many of the political issues of the time: Hitler and Mussolini flexing their muscles, running rings round Chamberlain and the appeasers, whose messy non-intervention policy hindered the legitimate government, but was ignored by the dictators. The whole tragic story of the inter-war left, so riven in the face of Fascism, in Spain showed moments of glorious unity. Today's students should not be surprised at CIA support for Pinochet in Chile and the Contras in Nicaragua when they learn that Texaco Oil and Firestone Tyres supplied Franco entirely on credit. The murderous technology of today's military was there in Spain: the bombing of civilians in Guernica and Barcelona—the latter by Italians based on today's holiday paradise of Majorca; and the German air support of ground forces in the Ebro battle. They even tried out and developed here the Messerschmitt 109, nearly as effective as the Spitfire in the Battle of Britain.

Within his brief compass Forrest manages to hint at another lesson: that there were many different wars in Spain—a fact perhaps true of all wars—there was class war between great landowners and desperately poor peasants; class war between capitalists and workers; anarchists, long influential in Andalucia and Catalonia, frightened liberal reformers; Carlists were still fighting nineteenth century battles over who should be king; agnostic liberals hated the Catholic church which saw its hold on education and women slipping away. Eventually these separate, yet interlocking, hates become engulfed in the tidal wave of the Second World War.

In part it is this volatile mix which produced the anger and bitterness of the 'Spain Days', something which is difficult to convey to present-day students, but an attempt should be made. We are given a quotation from de Foxá, whom Paul Preston called 'the régime wit', which opposes 'genealogy, race and prayers' to invading Russian tanks. In fact the first Russian tanks only arrived in Cartegena on 15 October 1936, three months after Germans and Italians had ferried virtually the whole of Franco's army across the Straits of Gibraltar. There were perhaps a dozen tanks just in time to contest the rebels as they approached Madrid in November. Perhaps a line or two of Auden's *Spain*, or some Antonio Machado would have given a balance.

So we have here the background, the parties and the personalities, the role of the International Brigades, and the key battles such as Guadalajara—where Mussolini's Italians were defeated by Government troops that included a battalion of Italian International Brigaders. We are reminded of Franco's paranoid hatred of 'reds', sometimes missing a military advantage in order to kill more of his enemies. His massacre in the bullring at Badajoz had an echo in Pinochet's Chile. Yet, surprisingly, there is no mention of Dolores Ibárruri—La Pasionaria . Although a communist, she became the outstanding symbol of resistance to Fascism. It was she who, as Franco neared Madrid in the summer of 1936, translated the French slogan from 1916 Verdun, 'They shall not pass' into the punchy Spanish, *No Pasarán*! After nearly forty years of exile in Russia, during which her son was killed at Stalingrad, and after Franco had died, she returned to Spain in 1977. When she died twelve years later aged 93, huge crowds jammed the centre of Madrid at her funeral.

Students today need to be made aware that echoes of the Spanish War still rumble down the years: when the war ended in March 1939 half a million refugees fled across the Pyrenees, ending up in Russia, Mexico and Britain (Portillo!) Thousands joined the French army and later the resistance; 12,000 Spaniards were imprisoned in Mauthausen concentration camp in Austria, of whom 7,000 died there. But in 1944 the city of Toulouse was liberated by mainly Spanish Maquis units and when the first French armoured half-tracks rushed into liberated Paris in August that year, their Spanish drivers had written on their sides 'Madrid', 'Guadalajara', 'Teruel' and 'Ebro'. Franco controlled Spain for thirty-five years, until he died in 1975 and was buried in a monument built by thousands of Republican prisoners. Only in the last few years have memorials to Republican dead been allowed.

Of course one could make some small technical complaints: perhaps I'm out of date on style, but what will sixth-formers make of 'disfunctionally broad spectrum'; 'accidentalist'; surely 'collaborated together' is a trifle pleonastic! Perhaps they will guess the meaning of 'alzamiento'; and why has the Gallic 'matèriel' crept in? I hope they will ask the meaning of 'libertinage'.

Although the terrible excitement of the 'Spain Days' does not quite explode on these pages, nevertheless Andrew Forrest has valiantly attempted to convey to a new generation the tortured history of those times—the first battles of a Second World War, which shaped the lives of so many. I do hope he is succeeding!

A.D. Atienza.
Retired teacher; formerly Curator of the International Brigade Memorial Archive,
Marx Memorial Library

Under the red flag

Keith Laybourn and Dylan Murphy, *Under the Red Flag: A history of communism in Britain* (Sutton, 1999), ISBN 0 7509 1485 8, xx+256pp., £25.00

Way back when the Research Assessment Exercise was only a gleam in the eye of university bureaucrats, it was conventional for authors to introduce their offerings with some explanation of their novelty and utility. This would currently appear highly appropriate in the case of work on British communism where the literature has recently expanded at an unprecedented rate. Taking broad surveys alone, the last decade or so has seen general histories of the Communist Party of Great Britain (CPGB) by Willie Thompson, Noreen Branson and Francis Beckett, as well as John Callaghan's volume covering both the CPGB and the Trotskyists.

No such customary justification is offered for *Under The Red Flag*, and in its absence we need to gauge the extent to which this text fills gaps and improves on its competitors. A new history may add to our understanding in a variety of ways. It may deploy new archival findings or personal testimony or foreground hitherto neglected aspects of the subject. It may freight familiar material with fresh insights, original interpretations or international comparisons. Or it may excel in its mastery of the terrain, the power of its synthesis, the quality of its writing, its rich rehabilitation of lost lives and its imaginative recreation of the past.

A preliminary issue is one of scope and focus. The book's subtitle and first chapter on Marxism in Britain before 1920 might suggest that it aspires to be more than a party history. This is misleading. The remainder of the text contains little on the ILP, nothing on the subterranean traditions of left communism and only a couple of pages on Trotskyism. Some 147 of 189 pages are devoted to the CPGB: it is on its treatment of this subject that the volume stands or falls.

In this context the first chapter provides a problem. It is intended to illustrate what seems to be—although other explanations periodically appear in the text—Laybourn and Murphy's central thesis. Their argument is that the CPGB's failure was ultimately bound up with the fact that it 'was formed too late to exert much influence on the trade union movement' and make good the deficit incurred by its predecessors, notably the SDF/SDP/BSP (p.xvi). There is certainly room in analysis of the CPGB for consideration of its political inheritance but here we are treated to an unfocused, diffuse and far from novel narrative. I remain unclear as to the relevance to the future CPGB's politics of the role of Bronterre O'Brien's supporters in the

SDF or the activities of Andreas Scheu and the Scottish Land and Labour League. Even in this over-expansive account there is repetition: Mark Bevir's views on the nature of Hyndman's support are retailed on p.9 and repeated on p.15. In contrast, matters of greater pertinence to what is to come, such as the BSP's affiliation to the Labour Party, are passed over in a sentence.

After a chapter which operates more as *excursus* than thematic statement of the problems bequeathed to the CPGB the party's creation is dealt with perfunctorily. The justification that it 'has been examined in enormous detail in other books' (p.43) would be more convincing were it not for the preceding 40 pages. The long-running but rarely explicitly confronted issues about the formation, nature and influence of the CPGB, perhaps most powerfully raised in Walter Kendall's *Revolutionary Movement in Britain 1900–1921*, are referred to by Laybourn and Murphy (pp.xv–xvi ,45–6). What one is looking for in a text like this is a sensitive statement of these issues and their complexity, without necessarily providing what will probably always remain contested answers. Here the Gordian Knots of socialist historiography are sparsely anatomised and then slashed through with the repeated assertion that, given the importance of the unions, the CPGB 'was formed too late to exert much influence on the trade union movement' and that it 'stood no chance of success, appearing, as it was, an anachronism in British politics once its forebears had missed its (sic) opportunities in the late nineteenth and early twentieth century' (pp.46, 189). In this brutal teleology Hyndman is more culpable than Stalin, to explore the history of the CPGB is to chronicle a death foretold. It was all over bar the shouting by 1920.

Determinism and reductionism constitute an underlying problem with this text. Hindsight, it goes without saying, is indispensable to the historian. It is a blunt-edged method which simply reads back what happened. It is a *sine qua non* for understanding that we also observe the situation in 1920–1 through the consciousness of its protagonists. They saw a world pregnant with possibility. They saw imperfectly: the balance of forces had already turned sharply against the working class, capitalism was stabilising, militancy was receding. The recasting of the labour movement, its closure against communism, the domination of labourism was unfolding. But it was contested. There was still space for revolutionary politics and their ultimate marginalisation was decided—and partly at least by the actions of revolutionaries—as the struggle developed; it was not determined by 1920. And if we hazard further that the CPGB should not have been established in the first place what was the alternative for revolutionaries? Kendall's suggestion that communists would have been better employed strengthening Labour's left wing is not explored here. It is attractive but it still begs the question, how? A more finessed approach to affiliation would still have come up against the Comintern and the 21 points. Organised entrism would have posed major difficulties. The impact of those who jointed Labour as individuals suggest unorganised entry would have done little to strengthen the left. Alternatively would an open party, liberated from Russian domination, have improved the prospects of the left? A variety of experiences, from the ILP down to the WRP and the SWP, suggest matters are not so easily resolved.

These questions are inadequately aired in a text which devotes more space to the Third Period than to the crucial early years of the CPGB. Despite the stress on the importance of the unions there is little examination of how trade unionists viewed the party or why so many joined and left. Regarding Kendall's assertion that the CPGB was 'an artificial creation' many would now accept that although the formation of the party, the form it took, the policies adopted, would not have been possible without the Comintern, the events of 1920–21 represented the genuine political impulses of British revolutionaries, however differently matters might be assessed as the 1920s progressed. Key aspects of the ongoing process of change, the consolidation of Comintern control, Bolshevisation, the implantation of the Leninist theory of organisation and struggle are discussed here briefly and blandly. For example, the Dutt-Pollitt report's aspiration to construct 'a party of a new type' is presented trivially in terms of 'getting rid of inactive branches', (p.48) rather than transforming the nature, site and impact on proletarian consciousness of revolutionary activism. Democratic centralism is not discussed until 1956 except incidentally. There is no consideration of the rationale, operation and impact of functional groups or party factory organisation. There is no new research.

Laybourn and Murphy's summary of the Third Period and the 1930s constitute the strongest section of the book and the authors talk good sense, if at times very general good sense, on the sustained subordination of CPGB policy to the Russians and the consequent subordination of class politics in cross-class alliances demanded by Stalinist foreign policy. But there is no attempt to absorb recent work, for example from Studer and Unfried and Thorpe and his colleagues, into closer analysis of relations with the Comintern. Kevin Morgan's finally chiselled distinctions between different periods of Popular Frontism are not developed. If Branson's over-sensitivity to the predicament of British Stalinism and Thompson's enthusiasm for the CPGBs entry into 'the political mainstream' are redressed, problems with the analytical framework remain. The party's progress is consistently measured somewhat artificially and absolutely against its ultimate yard stick of becoming a mass party and replacing Labour. Something less might have constituted success. International comparisons might have proved fertile. There is at times an attempt to cut through the complexities of why membership increased or decreased at different times by mechanical attribution to various political factors. For example, the Moscow Trials are depicted as 'horrifying' British workers and turning the hitherto productive link with the USSR into a negative factor (pp.xix, 92). There is little evidence for this. Indeed on the authors' usual indicator of progress the CPGB had by 1939 attained what was then and by a comfortable distance its highest ever membership while the zenith of pro-Sovietism was still to come.

The book's survey of the years of decline after 1945 is uneven. The section on the vital and under-researched early Cold War adds little to existing accounts. The CPSU Twentieth Congress and Hungary are accorded more detailed attention than the 1920s, while the emphasis is once more on what is already relatively well-documented—the oft-told revolt of the intellectuals—at the expense of the party's working-class base. Similarly there is nothing of substance on the CPGB's last significant success, what Thompson called its 'Indian summer', its activities in the unions in the 1960s and 1970s. It is ironic that a book which places such explanatory importance on the CPGB's failure in the unions examines so slightly key conjunctures when the party did make significant progress, such as 1941–8 and 1966–74. The final years of dissension and demise are, in contrast, accorded a generous 20 pages in an account which eschews reference to much of the burgeoning if scattered literature and simplistically portrays a bi-polar struggle between 'Stalinists' and 'Eurocommunists'.

There is the occasional similarity between earlier work and the authors' own statements. For example, on p.129 a passage describing communist successes in union elections is strikingly similar to a passage in Noreen Branson's *History of the Communist Party of Great Britain 1941–1951* (p.179) although somewhat surprisingly Laybourn and Murphy cite various issues of the *Daily Worker* as their source rather than Noreen Branson's book. The text is also prone to error. Palme Dutt is transposed from Oxford to Cambridge where he wins a first class honours degree. He edits the *Workers' Weekly* in 1922 although it did not replace *The Communist* until a year later, and spent his years abroad in Brussels and not, as indicated here, in Amsterdam. The non-conformist, if admittedly Jesuitical, J. T. Murphy is apparently at some stage received into the Roman Catholic Church in an example of premature Popular Frontism. Despite growing distance from his Scottish origins, Johnny Campbell still answers to the traditional appellation 'Jimmy', while Rust is dubbed 'Willie' by the authors, demonstrating a warmth and familiarity he inspired in few of his comrades. The Aircraft Shop Stewards National Council was formed in 1935, not, as stated here, in 1933. In the brief discussion of British Trotskyism there are at least half a dozen errors of detail. In any case, the judgement of anybody who recommends Volkogonov on Trotsky and fails to mention Deutscher must be open to question. Attfield and Williams, *1939: The Communist Party and the War* is commended to readers, but not the indispensable *About Turn*, edited by King and Matthews. There are several names misspelt.

Under The Red Flag is largely a macro-political account: it tells us little about communist people, the experience of activism, work in the regions, cultural activities. Judged on the criteria enumerated earlier, this text does not significantly improve on existing work. There is still a gap to be filled.

John McIlroy
University of Manchester

Stephen Woodhams, *History in the Making: Raymond Williams, Edward Thompson and Radical Intellectuals, 1936–1956* (London, Merlin Press, 2001), ISBN 0-85036-494-9, 221pp., £14.95 pbk.

Across a hundred years of dramatic change and upheaval, the two dates that bookend *History in the Making*, 1936 and 1956, remain among the most resonant of the twentieth century. For the left, in particular, these two years have significant import. On the one hand, the outbreak of the Spanish civil war and the varied responses to it in Britain and the wider world was a defining moment of the 1930s. It helped galvanise the struggle against fascism, and briefly forged a unity on the British left that has since prompted many a historian to view the late 1930s with a somewhat wistful air of what might have been. On the other hand, Khrushchev's secret speech to the twentieth congress of the Communist Party of the Soviet Union denouncing the worst excesses of Stalin, in tandem with the Suez crisis and the Soviet invasion of Hungary, combined in 1956 to facilitate an overhaul of existing political certainties and loyalties. Certainly, as anyone in attendance at the recent 'People of a Special Mould?' conference (held in Manchester, 6–8 April 2001) will testify, the episodes surrounding the Soviet invasion, not least the Communist Party of Great Britain's (CPGB) pro-Soviet response, remain an incredibly emotive subject for those who lived through them. Indeed, much ink has been spilt on issues relating to all these events—along with the small detail of the Second World War in between—and it is therefore Stephen Woodhams' approach to the period that makes *History in the Making* a very worthwhile and often insightful book.

Essentially, Woodhams compiles what he calls a 'collective biography' of certain British radical intellectuals over a period spanning from the 1930s to the 1950s, developing a 'contextual history' of the events (and institutions) that helped shape their respective political and theoretical actions and viewpoints. By so doing, Woodhams eschews 'traditional' biographical detail (birth dates, family, etc.) in favour of placing his subjects, particularly Raymond Williams, in the context of the epic events that occurred throughout the 1930s, 1940s and 1950s. Similarly, Woodhams focuses on the environments in which Williams and Thompson (along with others such as Eric Hobsbawm and Christopher Hill) functioned, most obviously Cambridge University, the Second World War, adult education, and the political, organisational and theoretical constructs of the CPGB. To this effect, Woodhams refrains from producing a history of ideas, and instead explains how, why and when Williams and Thompson formulated concepts and undertook initiatives that helped shape the history of the British left. In the author's own words,

> this generation which matured in the inter-wars years came out of a tradition of moral socialism formed during the nineteenth century…secular puritanism, voluntarism, commitment, etc.; vehicles through which it found expression included adult education, the Communist Party, the people's front and CND. (p. 22)

As such, Woodhams endeavours to situate his subjects within the more abstract notion of a British radical tradition, although he later concludes that this 'moral socialism' was unable to reproduce itself in the thoroughly different context of the post-Second World War world.

The fluid historical process outlined in *History in the Making* is one of the book's key strengths. By mapping changing conceptions, social structures and political alignments, Woodhams successfully demonstrates how ideas formed and developed, giving them a tangibility that is often missing from both biographies and general historical accounts relevant to these years. In order to do this, *History in the Making* follows a fairly chronological pattern, beginning with an overview of the 1930s and the principal events that helped forge the political perspectives of Williams, Thompson, et al. Thus, the widespread unemployment of the decade, the symbolic nature of the Spanish civil war, the apparent advances of the USSR, the initiatives opened up by the popular front against fascism (especially the Left Book Club), the supposed ineffectuality and passivity of the mainstream labour movement, and the limited but notable widening of access to Oxbridge that allowed those such as Williams and Thompson the opportunity to study at Cambridge, are all fused to explain just what gave an impetus to the left at this time. Likewise, of course, the onset of the Second World War impinged on Britain's radical intellectuals at a personal level, while also effecting changes to Britain's social, political and cultural structures. There is not the space here to chart the complex and varied experiences outlined by Woodhams. Very basically, however, he argues that as a result of such developments, along with the election of a Labour government, the implementation of welfare and educational reform, and the crude configurations of the cold war ('two camps'), Williams and, later, those gathered around *The Reasoner* in the CPGB, began to move towards the more cultural-based Marxist analysis of capitalism that eventually informed the New Left. Following the dramatic events of 1956, therefore, and under the Labour ratified shadow of 'the bomb', many on the left of British society began to search for new spaces and methods of political activity. For Woodhams, the publication of *Universities & Left Review* and the emergence of CND in 1957–8 marked 'both the end of asceticism and the beginning of a new manner of political behaviour in which neither the party nor anybody would take precedence over personal life'. (p.162)

Overall, Woodhams's argument is convincing, although it necessarily relies on generalisations with regard to the breadth of the changes to British society outlined throughout the book. Consequently, nuances, disparities and variations are sometimes lacking, and the focus of the book on mainly middle-class socialist intellectuals tends to neglect the fact that the Labour Party and the trade unions remained the principal focus of a workers' political allegiance, and that the CPGB remained a party led by and dominated by members of the working class. Again, the experience of the middle class socialist becomes the dominant historical narrative, so overriding that of the working-class activist. (For a similar point, see James K. Hopkins's excellent study of the Spanish civil war, *Into the Heart of the Fire: The British in the Spanish Civil War* (Stanford, 1998) p.5. But such minor concerns should in no way detract from what is an excellent and refreshing study. Woodhams's ability to pick his way through the unfolding events of 1936–56, and to then interweave the evolving perspectives of some of Britain's most influential intellectuals, gives rise to an informative and enlightening overview of a very dramatic time. By highlighting the context in which Williams et al. forged their ideas, *History in the Making* widens our understanding of the limitations, character and evolution of British radical thought.

Matthew Worley
University of Reading

Socialist History Journal

The *Socialist History Journal* explores and assesses the past of the socialist movement and broader processes in relation to it, not only for the sake of historical understanding, but as an input and contribution to the movement's future development. The journal is not exclusive and welcomes argument and debate from all viewpoints.

Other *Socialist History* titles

A Bourgeois Revolution?
Socialist History 1 · 1993
0 7453 0805 8

What Was Communism? Pt 1
Socialist History 2 · 1993
0 7453 0806 6

What Was Communism? Pt 2
Socialist History 3 · 1993
0 7453 08074 1

The Labour Party Since 1945
Socialist History 4 · 1994
0 7453 0808 2

The Left and Culture
Socialist History 5 · 1994
0 7453 0809 0

The Personal and the Political
Socialist History 6 · 1994
0 7453 0810 4

Fighting the Good Fight?
Socialist History 7 · 1995
0 7453 1061 3

Historiography and the British Marxist Historians
Socialist History 8 · 1995
0 7453 0812 0

Labour Movements
Socialist History 9 · 1996
0 7453 0813 9

Revisions?
Socialist History 10 · 1996
0 7453 0814 7

The Cold War
Socialist History 11 · 1997
0 7453 1241 1

Nationalism and Communist Party History
Socialist History 12 · 1997
0 7453 1267 5

Imperialism and Internationalism
Socialist History 13 · 1998
1 85489 107 3

The Future of History
Socialist History 14 · 1998
1 85489 109 X

Visions of the Future
Socialist History 15 · 1999
1 85489 115 4

America and the Left
Socialist History 16 · 1999
1 85489 117 0

International and Comparative Labour History
Socialist History 17 · 2000
1 85489 119 7

Cultures and Politics
Socialist History 18 · 2000
1 85489 123 5

Life Histories
Socialist History 19 · 2001
1 85489 129 4

Contested Legacies
Socialist History 20 · 2001
1 85489 135 9